PEOPLE MAGNET

The Art of Likability

Caleb Luke

CONTENTS

Introduction:

Social Brilliance 1

1: Front and Center 3

2: The Gratitude Effect 12

3: Power in Recall 22

4: Honor Your Opponent 28

5: Your Greatest Asset 38

6: Reviving the Dead 44

7: Head for Success 50

8: Navigating Conflict 58

9: Surrender to Egotism 68

10: Vulnerabilty is A Must 75

11: Mastery of Small Talk 82

12: Establish A Good Name 92

13: Others Before Me 101

14: Keep Your Hands Clean 107

15: Speak with Influence 116

16: Learn to Keep Your Word 124

Conclusion 131

References 134

Download the Audiobook for FREE

Want a free audiobook for **People Magnet - How to Talk to Anyone?** Sign up **free** for a 30 day Audible trial to receive it.

USA

UK

CANADA

AUSTRALIA

© **Copyright 2024 - All rights reserved.**

The content contained in this book may not be reproduced, duplicated or transmitted without direct written permission from the author.

Under no circumstances will any blame or legal responsibility be held against the publisher or author for any damages, reparation, or monetary loss due to the information in this book, either directly or indirectly.

Legal Notice:

This book is copyright-protected. It is only for personal use. You cannot amend, distribute, sell, use, quote or paraphrase any part of the content within this book without the consent of the author or publisher.

Disclaimer Notice:

Please note the information contained within this document is for educational and entertainment purposes only. All efforts have been executed to present accurate, up-to-date, reliable, and complete information. No warranties of any kind are declared or implied. Readers acknowledge that the author is not engaged in rendering legal, financial, medical or professional advice. The content within this book has been derived from various sources. Please consult a licensed professional before attempting any techniques outlined in this book.

By reading this document, the reader agrees that under no circumstances is the author responsible for any direct or indirect losses incurred as a result of the use of the information contained within this document, including, but not limited to, errors, omissions, or inaccuracies.

Special Bonus

Thank you for your purchase! We are exclusively offering the '30 Day Guide' PDF for free to say thank you for your support.

You will discover:

- 17 conversation starters to boost influence
- How to utilise social media for friendships
- How to strengthen relationships in 7 steps

Grab this FREE copy today. You can also sign up to my newsletter for free books, discounts, book releases and updates.

SOCIAL BRILLIANCE

Have you ever admired someone who effortlessly connects with others? They talk comfortably with strangers, command attention in a group, and radiate likability. You may have observed their body language, charm, and confidence in social situations, and you think they seem to have it all. Confidence is learned, not inherited. Our happiness is mostly dependent on our ability to get along with others. So, to succeed, one must possess the talent of talking to anyone about anything. The truth is we all need guidance on effective speaking and listening. Dealing with people is a big problem in everyday business and social life. And guess what? We all want to be influential and possess that undefinable quality that makes everyone fall in love with us. It can be challenging, but it is teachable.

I was never the best at talking to people. As a child, I dreaded speaking up in class. My teacher would call on me, and I'd stumble over my words, my face reddening as laughter arose. She'd sigh in disappointment and highlight the need for me to overcome my shyness if I ever wanted to make friends. I'd shrink further into my seat, feeling pitifully awkward and incompetent. It was a self-fulfilling prophecy—my discomfort around others perpetuated my isolation.

I am not alone in this. Ask around, and you'll find countless tales of social anxiety and fumbled conversations. Speaking confidently does not come naturally to most people. Building rapport and winning friends through dialogue is a skill that requires intention and practice. We must teach ourselves the techniques great communicators use to enjoy conversations while radiating likability.

Generic advice is not impactful, but this book will be. It will be your conversational blueprint for relatable discussions and wielding impact. You'll learn how to handle disagreements, establish trust quickly, become intriguing to others, and build strong relationships. Through framing and delivery strategies, you'll discover explicitly what to say and how to say it. Some are subtle, some are new, but all are attainable. You'll also learn when to speak, stay silent, and calibrate your emotional state from moment to moment.

You'll soon wield influence through the tool we use most in life—talking. We need a formula to achieve success in all relationships. You cannot force people to like you, but continuing to stumble through discussions blindly is no longer an option. So, embrace your incredible capability. The content revealed inside has already helped thousands lead more enriched social lives. Are you ready to make a change?

FRONT AND CENTER

You're on trial. And you have thirty seconds to make a great first impression. How did you do? Of course, after those 30 seconds, you still have countless opportunities to redeem yourself – if needed. Nevertheless, some of your personality is established by others in that time, even before you utter the first syllable. Quite frankly, people never accurately know your whole character at that time, but it does set the trajectory. They will warrant opinions of your character.

Guard your reputation. It could provide great power in relationships. So, while first impressions happen quickly, they make a substantial impact – whether the person assessing you is completely right or completely wrong. Your reputation is formed not just by how you act when eyes are on you but also when you think others are not noticing. Be confident when you talk to others, but do not be arrogant. Pair your confidence with humility by being open to learning from others and showing interest in their perspectives. The right balance earns respect.

PEOPLE MAGNET

I learned the potency of first impressions on my first day of high school when I transferred to a new town. I joined in Year 9, but all my other classmates were there since Year 7. I awkwardly wandered the halls, desperately hoping to make friends. I spotted a girl sitting alone in geography class and eagerly introduced myself. It turns out she was the popular girl. She gave me a slight look of disgust while turning up her nose and said, "You've got the wrong person." My face burned crimson as laughter broke out around us.

She made me feel unworthy of her friendship—with just one look. Unfortunately, my masculinity was bruised for a short moment. Her swift judgment deeply stung. I was front and center of an uncomfortable situation. So, I walked away, wishing I could re-do our introduction and better control the impression I made. But the damage was done; she never spoke to me again. I had fumbled my one chance.

Research affirms these experiences about split-second social judgments. Studies show people form first impressions within one-tenth of a second—even faster than the blink of an eye (Wargo, 2006). Those initial assumptions then act as filters, shaping how any new information about you is interpreted.

So, when you meet someone, be mindful that they are actively assessing your character. People judge based on appearances first; you must never be misled into believing otherwise because everyone focuses first on what is visible. Every element, from your clothes to your hairstyle, will contribute to the impression you make. These observations will be magnified when you are engaged in the conversation. Even if you're not directly interacting, observers nearby watch you closely and may scrutinise your conduct. You may also be surprised at how much of a conversation you understand, even if you never heard it. If you eavesdrop on any two people talking for just a few moments, you will easily create a quick overview of their relationship. You could tell if they were new acquaintances or platonic friends. You could also tell whether the two engaged in the conversation were in a romantic relationship.

Observers subconsciously note how you behave when you think no one is looking. It offers insight into the essence of your personality when you avoid putting on a show. As others observe you, they are not merely assessing superficial factors like your physical appearance – though this is crucial. Their primary focus lies in discerning signals related to your confidence and authenticity.

Let honesty be my virtue. Your reputation is also formed based on your associates and your impression on others impacts how receptive people will be to initiating conversations with you. Selective honesty is best employed on your first encounter with someone, but you must remain respectful while delivering your honest views. If someone knows you are honest from the start of the relationship, it will set a positive trajectory. One single act of honesty is insufficient - you must create a reputation built on a series of plausible acts. Consider that first impressions are not one-way; we, too, contemplate the intentions of others while meeting them.

PEOPLE MAGNET

Yes, life does have second chances, but reversing a bad first impression requires monumental effort. Essentially, your reputation is delicate. It takes perseverance to build up, but one mistake destroys it all. So, aim to make better ones. Conduct yourself in a respectable manner, and others will value your sincerity. Authenticity is key. Never pretend to be someone you're not. Speak your mind, but do so skillfully. As a wise teacher told me, "Truth without love is brutality. Love without truth is hypocrisy." So, voice your opinions, but with sensitivity.

People also quickly judge your character to decide if investing in you is worthwhile. Keep this in mind, for they take subconscious notes about who they believe you to be based on brief encounters. Nevertheless, be conscious of how you come across to others, and soon, you will possess a magnetic charm that draws people towards you effortlessly.

Reputations are built on the judgment of others, and this will influence your experiences in new social circles. A solid reputation will increase your likability, but you should also be observant of those who intentionally try to discredit it. A friend to all is a friend to none. Remember, there is no incentive when you neglect your reputation, so act with integrity, and you'll create a good name over time. A great reputation holds power in social circles, so guard it with your life. Once your reputation is damaged, you may experience attacks from all sides.

Let me illustrate this. You build a good name by strategically controlling the impressions you make during those first interactions. Again, you cannot force people to like you, but you must try at least to come across as sincere. I propose that you make your reputation simple by enhancing your greatest characteristic. So, let's imagine your greatest characteristic is your dependability. Strive to subtly show this to friends. Maybe you always arrive on time to your friend's run club on a Saturday morning, or you're known for keeping your word while under-promising and overdelivering. Maybe you're involved in the planning of your friend's wedding, and you've never not exceeded their expectations. Whatever it is – enhance it.

You must also come across as someone insightful. Someone who can add value to their lives—this will enhance your influence. Your reputation has the potential to cultivate respect. If you fail to care what others think about you, you let others decide. Adverse perceptions make getting to know someone less appealing, and when people believe they have accurately judged your character after initial interactions, they subconsciously seek out confirming evidence.

Your credibility influences how much weight others give your opinions. In social settings, warmth will increase your chances of being befriended. Professionally, showcasing preparedness and competence increases perceptions that you are capable. Learning to adopt behaviours that are specifically valued in a company is the key to maximising credibility. If your company wants you to be receptive in business meetings, give it to them. And if your company wants you to be more talkative in business meetings, give it to them.

PEOPLE MAGNET

My experience interviewing for my dream internship taught me how powerful initial impressions actually are. I was super qualified but also anxious and insecure. I stammered answers, slouched, and projected nervousness. Unsurprisingly, I was passed over for someone who made a great first impression despite having less experience. My awkwardness overwhelmed my credentials. I lost that credibility in minutes, which still haunts me today—I was seen as less capable. So, in later interactions, I worked hard to rebuild my image, but momentum was working against me. The unvarnished truth is that rebuilding is possible, but it will take perseverance. So, trying to get impressions right from the start is indeed recommended. Behaving authentically and considerately in public is salient. You never know what opportunities or relationships from those subtly observing you can create. Make a habit of acting with grace regardless of who is watching. Be the same person, whether in an observed public setting or alone in private.

On June 17, 1994, the most captivating car chase Los Angeles will ever remember climaxed. A former professional football player and beloved celebrity, once known for his charm and athleticism. OJ Simpson. The controversial name needs no explanation, but I shall give you one. His life took a dark turn in 1994 when his ex-wife, Nicole Brown Simpson, and her friend Ron Goldman were brutally murdered. The case gripped the nation as O.J. became the prime suspect in the gruesome double homicide. What followed was a high-profile trial that captured the world's attention. Simpson vehemently denied any involvement in the murders despite overwhelming evidence against him, including DNA evidence and a bloody glove found at the scene. The trial, often dubbed "The Trial of the Century," was marked by sensationalism, courtroom theatrics, and racial tensions. In a verdict that shocked many, he was acquitted of all charges in 1995. The shadow of suspicion will continue to make a lasting impact on him and American culture. The point of this story is this: We have all heard stories of prominent celebrities whose lifelong reputation was swiftly marred by a scandal or controversy. You may not be a celebrity reading this, but my point still stands:

Reputations are fragile

One mistake can cast doubt on years of good work. All the effort poured into presenting yourself as trustworthy, professional, ethical, and competent can unravel based on one false step in the wrong direction. Therefore, be vigilant about protecting your reputation. Be wary that your reputation is always on the line when meeting someone new. Do not take it for granted.

Authenticity must be your guiding principle. You never have to pretend to be something you're not when you behave according to your values. Sincerity and genuineness will always shine through when you stay true to yourself. Never be afraid of the characteristics that set you apart. Understand this: Trying to overly manipulate the impressions you make by putting on airs of charisma or even confidence can backfire and come across as disingenuous. People appreciate authenticity. That is the path to increasing likeability.

Furthermore, use inviting body language and utilise your conversation skills when meeting new people. Maintain an upright, open posture and establish eye contact. But also, be mindful of the latter. Increased eye contact can enforce a feeling of intimacy. Many know that exaggerated eye contact is compelling, especially between genders. And yet, prolonged eye contact is intrusive in some cultures. In some others, that same eye contact is an invitation for a fight and provokes a "What are you looking at?" response. So, use discernment when applying this advice. Surprisingly, to some, maintaining eye contact is great when speaking to confident people, but remember, intense eye contact feels hostile for those who are the opposite. Therefore, use selective eye contact – allowing adaptability to guide you.

Give a firm handshake – if needed. Speak clearly and loud enough to be heard. Ask thoughtful questions and share something about yourself. You must aim to guide the flow of the dialogue confidently. Again, it's important to display confidence, but it must be tempered with humility. So, admit when you're uncertain, compliment strengths you notice in people and express your appreciation for their time - these principles uplift others and keeps you from appearing arrogant. A little humility goes far.

Invite approachability and smile warmly - you want people to feel safe in your presence. Your conversations must be natural and executed with ease. So, ask friendly questions about their interests and experiences. Share amusing anecdotes that reveal your humanity. Your welcoming demeanour will motivate people to initiate conversations and forge connections.

FRONT AND CENTER

A few of my closest friendships started based on a conversation where they complimented my dress sense. A good tip to initiate conversations (especially if you love fashion) is to wear something unique or trendy that invites others to approach you and comment on your outfit. Simple, but it can work. Think about it, gentlemen. Suppose you're at a work event, and that one unique item catches the eye of an attractive woman across the room. If she fails to think of an opening line, she may comment on the item instead. I am sure you've engaged in a conversation where the first thing someone did was compliment you.

Also, follow social cues about proper conduct. Give enthusiastic compliments. React supportively when learning more about others. Master this equilibrium, and you will become great at initiating connections loaded with potential.

THE GRATITUDE EFFECT

In the bustling aisles of a vintage shop, amidst racks of retro clothing, I happened to notice a worker stressed and overworked. Max was his name, and as I browsed aimlessly through the aisles, I aimed to vocalise a characteristic that I truly admired in him. Often, offering a sincere compliment to a stranger can be daunting, but in this case, it felt effortless. With genuine admiration, I approached the worker as he hung the vintage hoodies on the racks. "Mate, what haircut do you ask your barber for?" I exclaimed with enthusiasm. "Your hair looks great!"

Taken aback, Max chuckled and looked up, his expression softening with gratitude. "Thanks, man," he replied, "I appreciate that." We later exchanged phone numbers and still used the same barber years later. Funny enough, I was back in the same vintage shop years later, but this time as an employee. Max was my line manager, and I secured the job through a referral program - all thanks to him. I had formed a close bond with him, all because I complimented him all those years ago. I installed the principle in high school to give creditable compliments - sincere ones.

He is now a trusted friend of almost a decade and as I reflect on my journey, I realised the powerful effect compliments have on relationships. Flattery driven by ulterior motives will fall flat. So, the secret to increasing likability is to show others how much ***you*** like ***them***. Again, it must be sincere. This principle, if applied correctly, could bring you countless friends and successful relationships.

Expressing gratitude requires an emotional vulnerability that may feel uncomfortable at first. Yet cultivating an attitude of thankfulness and conveying appreciation to others is profoundly important. Learn to make others feel great about themselves; become a source of comfort for them, and they will depend on your influence. Giving thanks from a place of true humility and wonder is no easy feat. We often feel shy when expressing heartfelt emotions. Keeping gratitude as a private feeling may seem easier than translating it into words or actions. And yet, it will serve no purpose if you want to increase your likability.

Putting gratitude into practice could be as simple as thanking the barista who makes your coffee daily or sending an email of appreciation to a helpful colleague. But even these routine expressions require intention and courage to break out of isolation. Each time we voice appreciation, we chip away at the barriers that separate us from others. Gratitude has the power to transcend suffering. To some extent, your success in relationships depends on your ability to value others, and it will pay you in dividends. So, empower those around you and strive to see greatness in them.

How can we reframe challenges as opportunities for gratitude? Perhaps we can thank friends for their support during a tragedy or appreciate doctors who eased a loved one's passing. Those acts of kindness become beacons in the darkness. Use the power of praise to awaken others' desire to excel.

There is often a tendency to overlook opportunities to express appreciation. Whether it's failing to acknowledge our children's success in winning a sports championship, neglecting to congratulate our spouses on their professional advancements, or overlooking our friends' achievements, such as passing a driving test. The virtue of appreciation tends to be undervalued in society. It's the reason why employees leave their jobs. The reason why a wife leaves her husband. The reason why athletes lost interest in the sport. Whatever it may be, it has significant consequences. Therefore, learn the principle: give sincere compliments.

Sometimes, opportunities arise where you wish to compliment someone absent. When that moment arises, consider indirectly conveying your appreciation through a trusted intermediary close to the person you wish to compliment. Allow me to elaborate on this strategy. Imagine you admire Noah's football skills. Rather than directly complimenting Noah, you could casually mention to Noah's housemate, Finley, something like, "You know, Noah is a remarkable footballer; I wouldn't be surprised to see him playing in the World Cup someday." Your remark will likely find its way back to Noah through Finley. Again, ensure the compliment is genuine and most importantly, credible. Understand this: I am not advocating deceptive strategies. I am talking about a new perspective to make great change. So, experiment with this approach if you wish. Not only does it evoke sentimentality, but it also mitigates suspicions of insincerity.

Andrew Cunanan was a criminal who gained widespread media attention for his murder of fashion designer Gianni Versace in 1997. Cunanan, who had a history of manipulating others and craving attention, targeted Versace as a high-profile victim in his quest for recognition and infamy. The crime sent shockwaves and garnered intense media coverage, fulfilling Cunanan's desire for notoriety. My point is this: the human desire for recognition can motivate positive and negative behaviour. Of course, the people you encounter are likely nothing like Andrew Cunanan, but discerning the intention behind praise and validation is still valuable.

There is a difference between sincere compliments and flattery. One comes from the heart, and the latter comes from the mouth. Be mindful of empty flattery to impress others. Insincere compliments come across as sycophantic. "That dress looks gorgeous on you" rings hollow if you have an ulterior motive. Those receiving over-the-top praise may feel manipulated and invalidated. Even just saying "thank you *for*..." to acknowledge kind gestures cultivates appreciation. No gesture is too small to merit sincere recognition.

PEOPLE MAGNET

Make it a habit to thank people. More importantly, make it a habit to thank people *for* something. Consider this scenario: You've just finished your tennis lesson, and as you bid your friend farewell, they kindly offer to drop you off at the train station. A simple "Thank you *for* taking the time to drop me off here. I really appreciate it" is advisable. Once you both arrive at the train station, taking a few seconds to express your gratitude can make a world of difference. Some people do this instinctively, while others do not. My attention is directed towards the latter group.

The longing to be recognised is not bad. Harnessed for good, it catalyses accomplishments. For instance, activists work tirelessly because they're passionate about the cause. More than personal glory, they desire societal recognition of the issue's importance; their yearning for validation aligns with their service. However, the desire for recognition can drive greed and envy. It's a double-edged sword. So, we must reflect carefully on our motivations to direct this innate need toward virtuous goals. With mindful gratitude and a desire for applause, we sow seeds of human potential. Society's aim should be to honour the best in one another through sincere appreciation.

I have a friend who exemplifies this principle beautifully. He had been dating a girl whose parents predominantly spoke Greek. He spent many months studying Greek, practicing the language at home, and attending cultural events to show his commitment. When he finally met her parents, he could converse with them in their native tongue. His efforts paid off and her parents were so moved that this man cared enough to learn about their origins.

THE GRATITUDE EFFECT

Not only did it strengthen his relationship with his girlfriend, but it also created a strong bond with her family that will last. His small act of taking the time to understand their background meant the world. Thankfully, the couple married years later, and her parents again expressed their gratitude for this commitment on their wedding day. They wanted all the guests to know his heartfelt impression on them. To them, his commitment spoke volumes about his character and devotion to their daughter.

Society craves affirmation. We want to matter to others, to feel that our presence makes a difference. Knowing that someone else holds you in high regard satisfies this core emotional need. Real fulfilment comes through relationships—family, friends, and colleagues—that affirm your worth. And the paradox is that to receive that appreciation, you must first extend it to others.

When you offer praise authentically, you make people feel uplifted. Rather than just completing rote transactions, take an interest in the lives of assistants, servers, and receptionists and elevate these routine exchanges into meaningful interactions. I must admit, the best way to increase likability and grow in confidence is to go out and do it. Some lessons are best learned when you take a leap of faith and pray for the best. Something as simple as "I appreciate you brightening my evening!" to a friendly barista can make their day.

At work, give credit where it's due. Thank colleagues who lent expertise on a complex project. Applaud team members for their contributions in meetings. Write handwritten thank-you notes to articulate specific, meaningful praise. The key is to let the other person know exactly what they have done well instead of using generic praise.

Compliment your spouse on how beautifully they care for your children. Let your child know you admire their concentration while practicing guitar. Look for those big and small opportunities to recognise people's shining qualities.

Want my advice? Do not offer excessive flattery that seems insincere. Generic praise like "good job" rings hollow without context. The most uplifting compliments offer explicit appreciation. So, help people see their strengths, the ones they may take for granted or feel insecure about. Making others feel valued also means avoiding criticism that erodes self-worth. Yes, constructive feedback said respectfully can help people improve, but resist the impulse always to improve your partner or micromanage your team. Focus instead on uplifting.

Personalised Recognition

Make people feel important, and they will respond rather well. Using someone's name makes them feel recognised as unique, not just a face in the crowd. Personalised forms of address, like nicknames, convey familiarity and fondness. Even small gestures of individualised appreciation strengthen bonds subconsciously by satisfying our fundamental need to feel valued. Dale Carnegie famously advised using people's names liberally in conversation. The sweetest sound for anyone is their name. It captures their attention and implicitly communicates, "You matter to me."

Get in the habit of greeting colleagues, clients, service workers, and so forth by name when possible. If you don't know their name, request an introduction or discreetly glance at a name tag, then repeat it during the interaction to reinforce it in your memory for next time. With closer friends and family, nicknames or terms of endearment demonstrate affection. A grandmother may have a unique pet name for each grandchild that binds them together. Romantic partners may call each other "honey" or "love." The moniker itself conveys the fondness of the relationship.

When used judiciously, individualised forms of address make people feel less anonymous and more cherished. Even in impersonal contexts like bulk emails, including the recipient's name personalises the content. "Dear John" feels more thoughtful than just "Dear Customer." That customisation makes a difference subconsciously, and it's also how large companies make big sales.

Likewise, handwritten notes feel extra meaningful in today's digital age because the writer took special care to individualise the message just for you. Handwriting the recipient's name and salutation extends the personal touch.

Giving personalised gifts also makes the recipient feel special—for example, an inside joke between friends, framing a photo from a shared memory, surprising your spouse with their favourite snack from their childhood. When you tailor gifts to every individual, it demonstrates how well you know them. And if you're honest with yourself, we all crave this type of individualised recognition.

Time Your Gratitude

Gratitude is conveyed in countless ways, but thoughtfulness around timing and methods will boost your impact. Rote habitual expressions lose meaning, while heartfelt words or gestures offered at pivotal moments deepen bonds. Consider when, how, and how often you articulate appreciation to optimise emotional resonance.

Timing influences the feeling behind thanks. Waiting weeks may make it seem like an afterthought. That immediacy can also backfire if it is not genuine. Reflexively saying thanks when opening a present, before you even see what's inside, comes across as empty. The most meaningful thank-you combine a timely response with tailored details on why you're grateful. For major accomplishments like graduations or weddings, handwritten congratulatory notes combines good timing with personalisation. They mean more coming promptly after the event when emotions are still fresh. Yet crafting a heartfelt message elevates a quick "Congratulations, great seeing you!" text.

For significant gifts, avoid letting too much time pass before reaching out. Follow up later with details, too; telling the giver how you enjoyed using their thoughtful present makes them feel rewarded long after. Timing also relates to frequency and context. Thanking your spouse for making breakfast daily may start to sound rote. Reserve those thanks for special occasions and smaller daily acts of service to keep it meaningful.

POWER IN RECALL

Recalling details about individuals is a must. Just as we desire others to listen to us and attentively remember our conversations, we must invest effort in doing the same. Our memory works best when we pay close attention from the start. Focus on what someone is saying rather than just waiting for your turn to talk. Getting the details correct from the beginning is the cornerstone for storing them in your memory later.

It also helps to make connections to things you already know. For instance, if someone tells you they love football, think of another friend who enjoys it. Or, if they name their dog, picture your pet. Relating new information to your past experiences creates reinforcement that helps the memory stick. Chances are better that you'll recall that someone adores football if you can imagine them cheering beside your best friend at a game.

Another good strategy is to imagine the details of an unusual or funny picture. This works more for some than others. The stranger the mental image, the more likely you will remember it. So, if a coworker says their favourite colour is purple, see them dressed in violet with purple hair and accessories from head to toe. You'll remember that preference if you can still see that vivid snapshot later. Again, depending on your learning strategy, this technique will prove more effective for some.

The Sweetest Sound

Tim Muller was not just any ordinary teacher; he was a master of names. He was known by his last name and over the years, he taught hundreds of students from all walks of life. Yet, he possessed an extraordinary ability to remember names after hearing them just once. Muller retained it in his memory no matter how complex or challenging the name. He understood individuals' profound importance of their names, recognising that their name was deeply tied to their identity. His remarkable gift cultivated an environment where his students felt truly seen and heard. They marvelled at his ability. It was no wonder that Muller was well-liked and deeply admired by everyone. Students admired him not only for his teaching prowess but also for his genuine care. In Muller's classroom, the power of a name was celebrated —a true testament to the great power of remembering someone's name.

Nothing puts a bigger smile on someone's face than hearing their name. Your name is more than just a word. From a young age, the sound of your Mom or Dad calling you is often comforting. As adults, we still feel acknowledged and respected when co-workers positively use our names in conversation. Incorporating their name in your vocabulary, like "It's nice to meet you, John," will warm their hearts – whether consciously or subconsciously.

Nicknames can also hold sentimental meanings from childhood. The personalised name your grandparents or best friend called you growing up may bring back happy memories. If you notice someone introducing themselves with an alternate name, it's fine to ask which they typically use or what their nickname means to them. Sharing the stories behind nicknames is a great way to learn more about someone on a personal level.

Remembering names is difficult when they are hard to pronounce - and this is where the majority fail. Most people would not attempt to recite people's names for it to become memorable. Instead, people ignore it or call the person by an easy nickname. People love to hear their names, so we aim to perpetuate it at any cost. Here's some free advice: Introduce yourself using your name and, in return, ask the other person for theirs; if you didn't hear their name distinctly, then apologies and ask them to repeat it. If their name is unique, ask them to spell it for you.

However, names and nicknames are used; be sure to say yours whenever speaking with someone new. Stating "I'm Caleb" upfront helps them associate a face with your name. Simple introductions create memorable impressions and aiding others' memory of who you are. An easy test is if they use your name when interacting again; that's a sure sign they were paying attention, and your name stuck—simple but quite powerful.

Practice introducing yourself, especially in chance encounters at social functions. Get in the habit of highlighting your name when able. Do not neglect the importance of this basic principle. If someone has trouble remembering your name or prefers a nickname, stick to the name you presented rather than switching to something different later. Keeping identification consistent helps solidify the connection between who **you** are and the name that represents you. Small gestures like greeting people by their preferred name or repeating them when saying goodbye go a long way toward making others feel subconsciously valued.

My daughter lived with a college roommate named Natasha, and she shared an insight into her upbringing with me. Natasha grew up in a toxic family where appreciation was often absent. Showing or vocalising any gratitude was alien to their lips. Natasha poured her heart and soul into her studies, driven by a relentless pursuit of excellence. Her family's toxic dynamics casted a long shadow over her accomplishments, and they never hesitated to belittle her achievements. Despite this, she graduated with a Doctoral Degree. What an achievement that was. She told my daughter about it, and I encouraged her to celebrate with Natasha. A few weeks later, my daughter surprised Natasha by arranging a celebratory meal alongside her other university friends. Initially hesitant about marking the occasion, Natasha enjoyed every moment. She continually appreciated the thoughtful gesture, underscoring the impact of feeling truly cared for and valued. This poignant instance exemplifies how attentiveness to details makes us feel recognised. Natasha moved to Canada shortly after, and they lost contact. That is a part of life. People come; people go. And yet, my daughter's impact will stay with Natasha whether she goes.

Remembering what someone shared shows we cared enough to focus on the meaning behind their words. When speaking with others, it's natural for our minds to wander occasionally to outside thoughts. But to absorb what's being said and to recall it later on, we need to force focus. Attentive listening greatly improves retention compared to passive listening with internal distractions.

Names, dates, or personal anecdotes are easier to recall later if we fully concentrate on grasping all context clues initially presented. These habits include setting aside any distractions like phones, maintaining eye contact, paraphrasing to ensure comprehension, and posing thoughtful questions. These actions will demonstrate attentiveness rather than mere superficial involvement. At first, it is mentally taxing to block out internal dialogue, but listening profoundly becomes second nature with practice.

Personalised Follow-Up

Staying in touch with others shows you were paying attention mindfully during past chats. One good way is to follow up with personalised questions about the things they mentioned before. Avoid underestimating this basic principle.

Imagine a coworker telling you last week she was attending her cousin's wedding over the weekend. A simple text a few days later asking, "How was the wedding?" would let her know you remembered that small detail. She'll appreciate the follow-through and be more likely to open up to you again, knowing her life updates don't fall on deaf ears.

Even casual acquaintances notice follow-up efforts. Something like commenting to the cashier at your local store that you hope her son is feeling better after she said he was hospitalised on your last shopping trip shows thoughtfulness. Remembering little things people share, even in passing, boosts relationships because it makes them feel heard. Tracking details through social media can also help you follow up naturally. If a friend posts photos from their at-home tennis game, ask them, "How'd your team do?" Commenting specifically about activities or experiences mentioned previously signals true investment.

Be sensitive when choosing what's worth a personalised check-in, as some topics are more personal than others. Follow your intuition when gauging what's meaningful while still being casual. Too many personal inquiries too soon could come across as overbearing. If someone opens up about serious issues, letting them know you're available if they ever want support is loving without demands.

Subscribing to casual follow-ups doesn't require much effort but does strengthen bonds. Remember, people appreciate being thought of, even through the smallest gestures.

4

HONOR YOUR OPPONENT

The golden rule is to remain respectful in disagreements and honour your opponent. Disagreements are inevitable in all relationships, as we have different opinions and perspectives. Diversity of thought can lead to growth, but disagreements can create tension and conflict if not handled reverently. It may surprise some, but you can express your viewpoint while still valuing the other person. So perhaps, we must develop the ability to sense problems when they are small and resolve the issues before they become intractable. My advice is simple: whether the issue is potentially disastrous or minuscule, never completely take your eye off it because it can re-enter your life with greater implications as long as it exists.

The unvarnished truth is that you must overcome the need to be right. First, begin any conversation in a spirit of goodwill rather than attack. For instance, say, "I have a different take on this. Can we talk it through?" Rather than, "You're completely wrong, and here's why," The first statement shows you're open to understanding their perspective, even if you don't agree.

Second, listen to understand, not to respond. Don't just think about what you're going to say next. Ask clarifying questions if needed. The issue with society is that we fail to ask probing questions that provide clarification. Assumptions can potentially destroy relationships, all because we forget to do one thing - ask.

Also, reflect on what you heard. "It sounds like you're concerned that my idea won't work because of X. Did I understand correctly?" You may notice the other person slowly becoming less defensive. You may have dropped their guard. You've shown them you've truly listened, and therefore, it cultivates an environment that brings down the guard of even the most adamant people. Essentially - you want to be a person of civility. This is one of the components to increase likability in all social circles.

Third, find common ground. Most disagreements are not black-and-white. So, try to identify points where you align. "I agree with your goal of wanting the best for the team. I have a different view on how to get there." Remain alert also to reciprocation opportunities. Finding common ground by adjusting your approach with everyone will greatly benefit all parties involved. Meet people where they are. If you make great efforts to study their perspective, you will get great results.

Fourth, stick to "I" statements rather than "you" statements. Say, "I disagree with that approach because..." not "You're completely wrong, because..." Using "I" statements explains your perspective without putting others on the defensive.

Fifth, remain open and flexible. Don't dig your heels in to win the disagreement. Consider other people's outlooks and be willing to incorporate any valid points. "You made a good point about X. I'll consider that." See where you can compromise without sacrificing your principles. I understand that, for some, this is incredibly hard to do - finding similarities in any disagreement is difficult.

Sixth, keep calm. Don't raise your voice or use abrasive remarks. Take a break if emotions run high. There is great strength in mastering your emotions; if you achieve it, there will be no limits to what you can accomplish. Unfortunately, getting overly emotional will only cloud your thinking and escalate tensions. Breathe deeply and stay focused on logically resolving the issue.

Lastly, end on a positive note if possible. Even if no agreement is reached, thank the other person for the open discussion, formally or informally. Suggest revisiting the issue later when you've both had more time to reflect. Agree to disagree. Get into the habit of distancing yourself from the present moment and think objectively about future repercussions. Patience is a skill. One that protects you from making miscalculations and one that provides opportunities for growth rather than divisiveness.

Here are some tips to keep disagreements from escalating into destructive arguments:

- Give people time to explain their perspective. Don't interrupt or get defensive - ensure you comprehend their standpoint.

- Ask clarifying questions instead of making assumptions. Get insight into why they think the way they do.

- Take a break if things get heated. Let everyone cool off before resuming the discussion; this has saved many relationships.

- Compromise where possible to find solutions everyone can accept. The absence of compromise leads to resentment.

Apologise sincerely when you're wrong. If you make a mistake, admit it gracefully. Do not create justifications for your actions. Avoid viewing disagreements as battles to be fought. Not every conflict is resolved immediately. Give yourself and others grace.

The secret to increasing likeability is showing compassion despite the circumstances. Most people seek sympathy in disagreements, so give it to them, and they'll love you. Learn to catch yourself when emotions rise and use calming strategies. That will be more profitable than division, as it cultivates understanding.

Respect for others, even when you disagree resolves conflicts constructively. Building bridges between differing perspectives allows you to navigate disagreements while strengthening relationships. It is essential to respect that everyone is entitled to their opinions. You do not have to agree with their stance but make it clear that you are open to hearing why they feel the way they do, this lays the groundwork for thoughtful exchanges.

Be aware of the impact of your words. Using inflammatory language is tempting for some but it immediately puts others on the defensive and it motivates them to prove you wrong. Comments like "You're being ridiculous" or "That makes no sense" will only anger and shut down dialogue. Instead, use unifying phrases like "I may be misunderstanding your perspective; can you help me understand where you are coming from?" This shows you respect their position and seek to find common ground.

Avoid condescending phrases that diminish others' worth or competence. Saying things like, "You should have known better" or "You always mess up" breeds resentment. Even if you feel someone made a mistake, don't attack their character. Focus on resolving the issue and use inclusive language like "We're in this together; let's figure out how to move forward." Use this strategy for relationships and friendships.

When tensions rise, consciously soften your body language and words. Maintain appropriate eye contact and an open posture to convey that you are fully engaged. Sometimes, we are too angry to speak, so occasionally, nodding shows we are considering their viewpoint without uttering a word. Mirroring their energy and tone helps create a harmonious exchange.

Finally, look for opportunities to find consensus. See if you can validate any part of their opinion. Being allies rather than adversaries diminish feelings of confrontation. Forgive others, too. However, do not let others take advantage of your constant forgiveness. Learn to set clear boundaries.

Disagreements are inevitable in all relationships. But if handled with mutual honour, they present an opportunity to gain understanding. You can discuss constructively without sacrificing your values by consistently respecting others' right to their beliefs.

Respectful and Disrespectful Language

Respectful language creates space for open dialogue. Here are some examples phrases that encourage constructive conversation:

- "I haven't considered it that. You've given me something to think about." Acknowledges their viewpoint brings insight.

- "It is clear we both want what's best for the team. Let's brainstorm together." Shared goals foster collaboration.

- "I have a different experience about this issue. May I explain my views" Different experiences adds helpful context.

- "I understand your feelings. My intent was not to offend. How can I express this more clearly?" Takes ownership.

Disrespectful language shuts down productive debate and harms trust. Here are phrases that can damage communication.

- "Wow! You're completely wrong and not making any sense." Dismissing their viewpoint disrespects them.

- "That's a stupid idea that would never work." Attacking ideas can feel personal and cause one to doubt their capabilities.

- "Why would you think that was a good decision to make?" Questioning their judgment breeds defensiveness.

- "Let me be honest with you because you are overreacting and being irrational." Accusations provoke anger.

Disagreements happen, but remember it may be hard to rebuild understanding once feelings get hurt. When people feel attacked, provoked or disrespected, they will defend their position more adamantly. So, admitting wrongdoing is key to overcoming hurt.

It's a natural reaction to retaliate when you feel your character or competence is questioned. If someone calls your idea ridiculous or implies you're incapable, you'll likely double down on defending yourself. In the heat of the moment, protecting your perspective takes priority over empathising with theirs.

This instinct to cling to our viewpoint only solidifies opposing sides. We stopped listening and instead planned our rebuttal. After emotions are involved, it becomes about winning the argument rather than understanding each other. Walls go up that block collaborative problem-solving. So, to steer things in a more positive direction after hurtful interactions, first, reflect on your role privately or publicly. Could you have phrased things less aggressively? Do you need to apologise for derogatory language? Taking ownership of miscalculations, even unintended ones, defuses tension.

Admitting wrongdoing may feel uncomfortable, but it's necessary for moving forward. Saying things like, "You're right; I should not have said that. I apologise for being dismissive of your feelings," opens the door to reconciliation. Be sincere without making justifications. You can also foster an environment of openness by thanking others for their patience and inviting them to share their perspectives. Comments like, "I know this is a sensitive topic; thank you for discussing it with me. I want to understand your viewpoint better," signals that you are letting your guard down.

Ask curious questions without judgment. Allow them to fully explain themselves before inserting your own opinions – do not dominate the conversation. Listen with empathy and reflect on what you hear. Building trust takes time after a conflict, but being vulnerable creates an opportunity for mutual understanding. Disagreements can strengthen bonds rather than break them when guided by a spirit of goodwill, not ego.

Giving Constructive Criticism

Constructive criticism requires finesse. Mishandling can bruise their pride and strain relationships. Think carefully about your motivation for giving feedback. Is it to help them improve? Or to vent your frustration? Criticism given out of anger is unlikely to be well received. So, make sure your intentions are honourable.

Next, timing is key. Don't criticise someone publicly or when emotions are running high. Wait for a private moment when both or all parties are calm. Beginning with praise also helps soften the blow. For instance, "You have always designed such creative presentations, and I have a thought that could make this one even stronger." Use the power of praise to awaken their desire to excel.

When sharing critique, focus on the issue rather than the person's character. "I think this report would benefit from more detail" differs from saying, "You're bad at writing reports." The former centres on enhancing the work, not attacking the individual. Use gentle yet direct language.

Don't downplay or sugarcoat what needs improvement; instead, communicate it compassionately. For example, "I noticed several grammar errors that detract from the professionalism of the document." Straightforward but not accusatory. Explain exactly why a change is needed and how it will help. Do not underestimate the power of this because vague disapproval without concrete suggestions leaves the person confused and discouraged. Always provide actionable steps tailored to their situation.

After giving feedback, check for understanding and invite open dialogue. Create space for the person to ask probing questions, offer their perspective, and feel heard. Adjust if your guidance does not work for their circumstances.

Finally, end on an encouraging note by expressing confidence in their abilities. For example, "I know you can take this presentation from great to exceptional by making these few tweaks." This motivates improvement while still validating their work so far. Constructive criticism should not harm self-esteem or

HONOR YOUR OPPONENT

relationships, so when given skilfully, it reveals your commitment to their development. Ensure your words uplift and enlighten.

YOUR GREATEST ASSET

The renowned advice to greet people with a smile was popularised in Dale Carnegie's 1936 classic "How to Win Friends and Influence People," it rings true over 80 years later. While it's a simple act, a smile makes a profound impact, one that conveys warmth and approachability. Grinning is not enough. Smiles must be infused with authenticity to be impactful. In Carnegie's time, flashing one's pearly whites, whether genuine or not, was encouraged as good etiquette. But now we demand sincerity. Just arranging your mouth into a grin lacks magnetism. True smiles crinkle the eyes and brighten the whole face with sincerity. Joy reflected through your entire essence is contagious.

Those excelling socially know a sincere smile carries power. A lot of power. So, when utilised strategically, it instantly creates trust and draws others in. The absence of a smile radiates coldness, and a deceitful smile questions your intent. So, if you don't feel like smiling - force yourself to. People rarely succeed at anything without a smile. So be the one to uplift spaces through yours. Try a slow smile if you wish to impact everyone you meet considerably. A slow smile will be your biggest blessing if used correctly. So, to the next person, you greet, pause, maintain eye contact for a few seconds, and then smile. It will warm the heart of the other person. That small delay will convince the recipient that your smile is real — personalised just for them.

While smiles should be sincere, we should also know there are opportunities to use them, so be alert to them, like greeting shop workers, mingling at events, chatting with colleagues, and passing strangers. Those brief acts of silent kindness open doors to fulfilling relationships.

At a prestigious business event in Chelsea, London, my fiancée at the time was determined to secure another joint venture. She was the quintessential example of beauty and knowledge; she strode confidently into the room, ready to make a lasting impression on everyone she encountered. However, despite her best intentions, few approached her. Why? Well, her unintentional display of a resting face radiated bitterness and disinterest. As she attempted to socialise with the crowd, her features unveiled none of the warmth and enthusiasm that bubbled inside her. Instead, her expression remained stoic and impassive, unknowingly sending out signals that repelled potential opportunities.

The power of a smile, my fiancée soon realised, was not to be underestimated. It was a universal language that transcended barriers and forged instant connections. At that moment, she failed to grasp the profound influence of utilising a sincere smile to bridge the gap between herself and others. We reflected on the missed opportunities of the evening, and she vowed to approach future interactions with a new understanding of the influence of her demeanour.

Remember, in most interactions, we receive the energy extended. When approaching others positively, few reject polite goodwill. Therefore, begin each encounter with an open heart and an optimistic spirit. The world tends to mirror what we project, so allow your zeal for people to grow through cheerful smiling.

Understand this: People discern between smiles that beam from the heart versus polite grinning. Genuine warmth and joy from that one smile can build rapport. But faking smiles out of social obligation will backfire, as it appears manipulative. Strive for authenticity. Those formulaic tips to always smile persist from earlier eras; that advice requires nuance today. Insincere smiles are shallow. A smile that emanates from the heart holds great power in social circles. Sincere expressions of joy have the most magnetism for forging connections. A warm smile is one of the most universally effective tools for breaking the ice.

Rather than immediately launching into verbal communication, lead with a smile when initiating contact with unfamiliar people. Its raw authenticity speaks volumes and welcomes people to engage with you without demanding a response. Smiling breaks down social barriers and paves the way for more dialogue by displaying your benevolent intent.

A smile humanises you and assures strangers you come in peace. Its charm short-circuits negative assumptions and it makes others feel at ease, so if you want to be a people magnet, let this be the way forward. Smiling is confidence balanced with humility. You become someone people want to know which shifts dynamics in your favour.

Once a smile has broken the ice, strangers often instinctively smile back. this builds a bridge between you both. Now, a friendly verbal exchange can develop from your nonverbal overture. Smiling signals, you are worthy of their trust. When approached first with a warm smile, people tend to reciprocate that friendliness.

As a predominantly nonverbal cue, smiling has advantages over verbal icebreakers. Why? Well, its sincerity is harder to fake and, therefore, it is powerfully persuasive. So, learn to train your discernment skills by noticing how authentic smiles are in social and professional interactions. And since authentic connection is highly valued today, perceived fakeness damages your reputation. Smile with intent, but keep it real. Sincerity and goodwill should never be faked.

Smiling at Friends and Strangers

A smile is often natural when directed toward loved ones. It takes no effort—in fact, it's instinctive. Warmly beaming at dear friends is instinctive. But resist confining your smiles only to those closest to you. Look for opportunities to spread smiles broadly among acquaintances, colleagues, neighbours, service workers, and rude strangers (yes, they sometimes deserve love too). Extend goodwill to all through this simple gesture. A society that smiles eases isolation and empowers belonging. Overcome assumptions that those outside your inner circle don't warrant a smile.

These are some examples of appropriate smiling moments:

Greeting a neighbour in the morning: Whether exchanging waves across the street, nodding in the driveway, or passing in the hall, greet your neighbours with a smile. This harmless courtesy, when reciprocated, makes communities kinder.

Meeting a colleague in the workplace: Warmly smiling when interacting with coworkers, even if you don't know them well, promotes goodwill and approachability. Don't underestimate the team-building power of a simple smile.

Passing by a stranger on the street: Briefly smiling at those you pass while out reinforces our shared humanity. A quick, sincere grin at fellow pedestrians, motorists, or cyclists opens possibilities for surprising moments of connection.

Engaging with a cashier: Service workers bear the brunt of rudeness all day. Effortlessly smiling, expressing thanks, and wishing them well as you checkout can tremendously brighten their day.

Everyone believes smiling is common sense, but few people do it. Smiling without an agenda will powerfully transform your social

YOUR GREATEST ASSET

interactions. So again—let your smile be your greatest asset and use it for maximum effect.

REVIVING THE DEAD

At the age of 20, I worked at an estate agency in Manchester, United Kingdom, where I was temporarily supervised by Sarah and Mark, who, after acquaintanceship, embarked on a romantic journey with their inaugural date at a wine-tasting bar. They were polar opposites. Mark's sanguine demeanour secured property deals, while Sarah, known for her quiet nature, excelled in negotiation. I suppose the saying holds true - opposites do attract. And yet, their initial date did prove somewhat uncomfortable, and word of it swiftly circulated throughout the office. Mark, increasingly preoccupied, checked his phone often while Sarah's attention appeared to drift, and her responses grew more reserved. Mark became embarrassed as he struggled to inject energy into a dull conversation to appease Sarah. Despite their attempts to maintain momentum, the dialogue faltered, punctuated by awkward pauses and strained efforts to sustain engagement. Their once vibrant exchanges in the office gave way to a palpable sense of disconnection.

We've all experienced those awkward moments when a discussion starts to deteriorate with nothing left to give. Noticing when interactions begin to lose steam is a powerful ability, as is knowing how to get things flowing again smoothly. A few telltale cues show interest may be waning: bodies shift further away, eye contact breaks more often, and responses get shorter with less elaboration. Phones may casually appear for checking as minds wander elsewhere. Silences that were once comfortable now feel strained. Once these signals align, it's a good hint to steer things in a livelier direction.

Listen for verbal signs, too, like repetitive, vague filler words ("umm" or "you know") rather than descriptive language. One-word answers that don't invite follow-up questions are another signal. If you notice yourself automatically doing these things, it's time for a shift. Don't be afraid to gracefully acknowledge a low point with humour by commenting, "This chat seems to be losing steam. Can we talk about something else?" with a smile to release tension. Remember not to make a joke at someone else's expense – avoid attacks on someone's character.

Jumping right into asking numerous questions often backfires by putting pressure on the other person to do all the talking. A better strategy is to offer your own observations or stories to get the ball rolling naturally again. So, recall past discussions and probe for updates. Try bringing up recent news, funny experiences, or cultural happenings you think they'd find interesting. My personal favourite is posing a hypothetical to spark creative what-ifs. Indirectly taking the initiative can re-energise all parties.

Don't force it if all else fails. Simply conclude the interaction pleasantly rather than dragging on a dead horse. The art lies in subtle yet engaging tactics that make others think you've brightened the exchange organically. Ultimately, it's about sparking interest, not salvaging failures.

Having a discussion lose steam is nothing to stress over. It happens to all of us at times. Nonetheless, make it a habit of acknowledging the signs of a boring conversation and enliven it. If possible, gently shift topics to something more engaging by relating them to a prior discussion. Say something like, "You mentioned your holiday plans—did you go to that new restaurant you saw advertised?" This transitions naturally rather than seeming like an attack. Bringing up a shared interest, current event, or funny experience you think they'd find interesting also redirects positively. Try it and see if it works for you.

Offering your anecdote can inspire others to open up more since they're not put on the spot. Say something self-deprecating to lighten the tension, like, "Man, you would not believe the dumbest thing I did the other day trying to fix my car." Sharing in a down-to-earth way often prompts reciprocal sharing versus tons of intrusive questions. Comedy also tends to breathe life into fading interactions by releasing pressure.

If refreshers aren't bringing the person around, don't force it. Acknowledge it and walk away. So, with a compassionate smile, say something like, "Well, I don't want to take up too much of your time. I'm glad we could catch up a bit, though. Take care!" This leaves people wanting more. A brief parting reminder that you're available if they want support shows that you truly care without demands. Sometimes, energy isn't there, so no hard feelings.

Also, be attentive to micro-signals of discomfort. Have confidence that, with relational skills, you can navigate highs and lows fluidly. A dead interaction can transform into a chance to deepen rapport. Keep this positive mindset; revitalising discussions will soon feel as natural as enjoying great ones.

Assess Timing and Know When to End

One mark of a considerate conversationalist is understanding when it's best to gracefully exit an exchange before it starts to drag or lose steam. A keen sense of timing is fundamental in leaving on a high note. So, pay attention to signs indicating tiredness, such as frequent yawning, glancing at a watch or phone often, or fidgeting restlessly. Taking more time to reply, one-word answers, or not contributing much beyond short acknowledgments are signs of interest waning. While you are chatting, monitor energy levels to recognise when to conclude before things begin to decline visibly. Sometimes, you must leave people wanting more.

It's also good to be conscious of how long the interaction has lasted. Standalone coffees or quick chats in passing have a natural brevity, while deeper check-ins with close friends can comfortably run longer. Know yourself and the other person's personality, too.

Remember, some thrive on brevity, while others enjoy prolonged dialog. Tailor based on context clues.

Choose your exit time wisely. When things are still upbeat, it is ideal to leave on a positive note. If the conversation takes a more serious turn, allowing some laughter or a shared smile before departing reassures that the bond remains strong regardless. Socialites know not to reveal everything at once. That sense of curiosity intrigues others, as your unreadability often attracts people to you. The art of controlling your tongue and monitoring what you reveal enhances your conversational potential.

Subtly watch external queues that affect the environment as well. If places become noisier or more crowded as time passes, it's respectful not to overstay your welcome. Reading such evolving room dynamics prevents imposing beyond a comfortable setting. Social awareness enhances interactions. It's a myth that lengthy chats improve relationships. Respect others' time and your own.

To wrap up tactfully, reflect on a high point you connected over and briefly highlight, hoping to connect again soon before saying farewell. Short positive texts after, like, "It was great chatting tonight; have a good rest of your day!" still convey care without prolonging beyond prime momentum. Mastering cheerful exits leaves interactions feeling purposeful and pleasant. Positive perspectives also liven exchanges. Try to get into the habit of framing experiences or opinions constructively rather than with bitter cynicism. Most importantly, interactions with the other person should be made through engaged listening and frequent questions rather than monologuing. You must prioritise understanding what matters most to them. Society does prefer genuineness to superficial showcasing.

Engagingly connecting with others comes down to more than just chatting. It's displaying likable traits that paint you as a truly fun person to be around. Good conversationalists know how to showcase qualities through dialogue that leave listeners feeling uplifted. One trait that fun talkers exhibit is a playful sense of appropriate humour. Not clowning around constantly but inserting light-hearted quips or smiles at appropriate times that keep exchanges lively versus heavy. People are naturally drawn to those who can find humour in everyday things.

Part of coming across as an entertaining talker is enthusiasm. Folks feed off the good vibes of those visibly enjoying simple exchanges. Dull or monotonous dialogue grows tiring for listeners. People magnets implement likable qualities that transform even mundane exchanges into uplifting ones that people remember fondly. Knowledge of diverse subjects prevents conversations from becoming too narrow or one-dimensional. Versatility leaves others feeling you can connect with their interests as much as your own.

Approachability is paramount. Share vulnerabilities or quirks subtly to make interactions feel easy-going without macho fronts. Admitting minor embarrassments invites listeners to let their guard down and bond through relatability. Fun people seem real versus those who strive for perfection.

HEAD FOR SUCCESS

A good conversation is sweet – and good conversationalists are heading for success. Often, people are viewed as likable because they have mastered the art of talking to anyone about anything. They can balance talking and listening. Make sure the conversation doesn't become one-sided. Don't go on and on about yourself without letting others contribute. Read social cues about when to draw back and when to speak up. Bring liveliness and wit. Use humour appropriately, and share interesting anecdotes – if needed that add colour to the conversation. But don't take over with overly long stories or jokes that may bore others. Read the room.

Reciprocation is a two-way street. So yes, you must also put the effort in. To thrive in any social interaction, becoming a people magnet will require reciprocation. Society intuitively longs to feel acknowledged and validated. Demonstrating you are interested in someone more than being interesting to them draws people magnetically toward you. A component of effective reciprocation is active listening. Many fail to increase their likeability because they do not listen attentively. Sometimes, you'll find that people talk constantly to unburden themselves. They rarely want your advice. Just a sympathetic listener who shows their attentiveness.

Correct delivery of words is also essential. Doctors inform their patients they need chemotherapy with compassion. Parents inform their children they need their wisdom teeth removed with consideration. Interviewers inform potential candidates they were unsuccessful with sympathy. I'm sure you get the point, yet most people are unaware of the sensitivity needed.

On another note, new people most likely won't grasp your personality enough to put your foible into context. Once the relationship has solidified, telling your new friend that you were arrested before, ran away from home, or quit on your first day at university may not be a massive problem. However, I can place a bet that if you said that exact information on the first day you met them, they would have been sceptical of you.

Here is one word of warning: do not reveal too much too fast. I have witnessed countless conversations spiral from someone becoming too transparent too quickly.

Here is a controversial take. If you are already established in a group, sometimes use your occasional absence to make others realise your impact. Friends will appreciate your presence more as it will become more valuable. You may be forgotten if you withdraw too early and for too long. Everything depends on your absence and presence. The potential brilliance of this technique is that once you've returned to the group, it will be as though you had come back from the dead - an air of resurrection. Nevertheless, you should practice this with caution and care.

Steer away from sensitive topics like politics, religion, or personal finances unless you know the other well. Consider universally engaging subjects around current events, pop culture, travel, and more - based on your common interests. This could get boring after a while, so adjust it when needed.

Many people are open books, but people magnets rarely reveal everything at once. Curiosity intrigues others to learn more about you through further conversations; your unreadability attracts people to you. The art of controlling your tongue and monitoring what you reveal will enhance your conversational potential.

When we engage in the inevitable small talk - master it and then develop it so you become a dynamic conversationalist. Asking probing questions and attentive listening are the cornerstones to perfecting dialogue. Above all else, people are interested in themselves, so when you demonstrate a sincere interest in learning about someone, it makes them feel appreciated. Attentive listening reinforces that their perspectives are important to you. Mastering these skills will be a great asset to you.

My advice is simple: you should move beyond superficial small talk and have a substantive exchange. Go beyond polite tendencies like, "How are you?" to queries illuminating who they are. "What projects are you working on currently?" "How did you get into that field?" "How did you find growing up in a big town?" Open-ended questions invite people to share as much or as little as they wish.

Listen carefully to their responses so you can ask relevant follow-up questions. If they mention a major accomplishment, ask, "What challenges did you face getting there?" If they name a city, ask how long they have lived there. Active engagement ensures the conversation flows. A great conversationalist knows people.

So, avoid questions that can be answered with just yes or no. Those often shut down opportunities for storytelling. Beyond specific questions, cultivate an attitude of wanting to learn from every person you meet. See each interaction as a chance to gain a new perspective. Give your full attention when others speak. Maintain eye contact and positive body language. Avoid distractions and multitasking. Don't formulate your response while they are talking; just concentrate on comprehending.

Discreetly repeat the keywords and phrases they used to emphasise that you're absorbing their narrative. Comments like, "That major achievement you mentioned…" or "Going back to your point about the challenges…" show precise listening. Learn to vocalise complete sentences to show your understanding. Avoid vague filler words and replace 'Umm' with a simple 'I get what you mean' or 'Oh, that makes sense.' These small changes add a sentimental element to the conversation, and it encourages the speaker to reveal more out of confidence.

Mastering the art of asking and listening well will transform your conversations. What distinguishes an engaging conversationalist from a boring one? More than skill or wit, it comes down to sincere interest in others. People magnets are as fascinated by humanity as they are by being heard.

Consider Oprah Winfrey's undeniable conversational superpower. She intently listens with presence and empathy. By getting guests to open up, she uncovers relatable human experiences. That is what created her success. As she says, "I have a lot of questions. If I'm the question, then the guest is the answer." Her curiosity creates intimate connections.

Or take renowned interviewer Terry Gross, host of Fresh Air. Her methodical research and impromptu follow-up questions coax fascinating stories from thousands of guests. She doesn't force conversations into preconceived notions but instead, she follows the other person's direction.

Good conversationalists share their own thoughts, too, just selectively. As the adage goes, "Better quality than quantity." Don't immediately offer strong opinions before understanding the context. Consider timing and language before asserting your views. For instance, "You make fair points. May I offer another angle to consider?" rather than "You're wrong. Here's what I think." And don't stay attached to initial opinions if the conversation evolves. Adjust the conversations based on new insights. Speak with clarity and confidence without dominating the volume. As author Keith Ferrazzi notes, "Loud, boisterous talkers are often covering up their own sense of inferiority." Trust that your ideas can speak for themselves.

Connecting with others starts by appealing to their interests. This timeless concept, derived from Dale Carnegie's influential book, "How to Win Friends and Influence People," remains relevant. Carnegie stressed the wisdom of taking a sincere interest in others. "You can make more friends in two months by becoming interested in other people than you can in two years by trying to get others interested in you."

So, ask people about themselves and their lives. Listen attentively to their responses to identify common interests; conversational opportunities naturally arise. So, if someone mentions they coach football, ask about their most fulfilling coaching moments. Share that you enjoy playing football recreationally. Now, you want to discuss football skills, World Cups, favourite players, and more.

Don't just wait for common interests to emerge randomly. Research the people and groups you'll interact with to identify shared interests proactively. If you chat with another parent at a school event, ask about their kids' ages, grade levels, and teachers.

Carnegie also advised using people's names in conversation. The sweetest sound for anyone is their name. Calling others by name signals that you find them important. Nicknames can hold even greater power. Beware of spending too much time on your own interests rather than pursuing others. Be more curious than self-focused. Again, people are, above all, interested in themselves. Carnegie also stressed sincerity. Feigned interest is obvious. Truly care about understanding what makes people act the way they do.

In our digital age, a quick online search can uncover people's passions before meeting in person. The principles are timeless.

Boring Conversations and Adjustments

Riveting conversations requires awareness and agility from all participants. Changing course politely is important if you sense that the other person is losing interest. Look for subtle signs of boredom and adjust your approach to re-engage them. With care, you can redirect dull interactions into dynamic exchanges. What are telltale indicators that your conversation is boring for others? Frequent checking of a watch or phone is an obvious clue. But also note fleeting eye contact, tapping fingers. Is their gaze wandering instead of staying focused on you?

Listen for verbal signs, too. Is their speech becoming monosyllabic instead of substantive? "Uh huh" rather than "That's fascinating." Are they giving obligatory but empty praise like "sounds good" instead of specific feedback? Don't ignore these red flags. If you stay oblivious while they disengage, the conversation will sputter. You may feel awkward, too, as momentum dies. Be proactive in reenergising the interaction – if needed. How? Gently interrupt to shift focus. If you've been dominating about a topic they're bored with, pivot to ask about their interests. "On another note, what projects have you been working on lately?"

Inject thought-provoking observations to stimulate discussion: "That reminds me of something interesting I read recently." Introduce new perspectives without seeming scattered. Sprinkle in timely humour to lighten the tone, but avoid overdoing it. A few amusing anecdotes can work wonders to regain lively energy.

NAVIGATING CONFLICT

Daily, we engage with many people – friends, family members, colleagues, supervisors, and even strangers such as shop cashiers. And so, conflicts inevitably arise on occasion. It's only natural for people to see things differently and have different opinions. Most arguments end with both or all parties feeling more confident that they are completely right and the other person is completely wrong. Many people also look for sympathy in arguments; give them it, and they will love you.

Let's acknowledge that conflicts are normal. As long as two or more people talk, differences are bound to surface. We all have unique experiences, beliefs, and perspectives that shape how we see the world. So, expecting everyone to think the same on every topic is unrealistic. Our differences are what make discussions interesting. But they also leave room for the possibility of friction.

Conflicts arise because people place importance on different issues. What one person sees as very important; another may see as less so. Differing priorities can lead to opposing views. People also have diverse communication preferences that may not always align. While some favour a direct approach, others prefer a gentler conversational tone. The clash of opposing styles alone generates tension, regardless of the significance of the topic at hand.

Fights are also more likely to erupt when certain moods and emotions arise. We are humans of emotions, not logic. So, if someone feels irritated, tired, or stressed for other reasons, they may react more strongly to a disagreement than usual. A point that could be discussed calmly on a good day may trigger a heated argument when patience is running low. Our energy levels and circumstances colour our responses.

Understand that conflicts exist on a spectrum. Not all discrepancies are major blowups. Plenty of everyday quibbles are over tiny details, like choosing what to eat for dinner or whether to see an action or comedy movie. Trivial quarrels don't last long once a small decision is made. Less dire conflicts are opportunities to practice resolving issues smoothly. On the other hand, deeper-rooted clashes require extra care and compromise to resolve.

A golden rule is to praise in public and criticise in private. If you must criticise the other person in an argument, call attention to your faults first and always provide solutions. Avoid mentioning the criticism more than once, deliver it sensitively and hope change will come from it. A good practice is circumventing the word **'but'** because it cancels out everything you said before that - use the word **'and'** instead.

Disagreements are rarely about right versus wrong but about differing perspectives. Rarely does one side have an absolute monopoly on the correct view. Good-faith disputes stem from multiple rational standpoints, not stubborn refusals to accept the truth. Realising this prevents the needless assigning of blame.

The truth is that it gets increasingly harder to change people's opinions after you've insulted them. Yet, conflict avoidance can leave underlying problems festering to explode another day. Airing views openly after establishing respect allows for deeper understanding. Compromise becomes possible when each side grasps the reasoning behind the other.

Nevertheless, conflicts will grow nasty when civility departs and personal attacks replace factual discussions. Name-calling, harsh accusations, bringing up irrelevant past actions—these behaviours poison the environment, and a resolution becomes impossible. Once you're in an argument, stay polite and address only the present issue to keep interactions constructive. Master your emotions, too, as they overshadow reasons. Learn to distance yourself from the present moment and think objectively about future repercussions. Patience is a skill. One that will protect you from making miscalculations.

When conflicts arise in conversations, most people's first instinct is to focus on being right and prove the other side wrong. But this often creates resentment and makes other people strive harder to prove you wrong. Again, we must remember that we're all humans, meaning we run more on feelings than anything else. How we think and respond is coloured by our emotions, for better or worse. If your goal is to resolve the argument instead of just winning it, you must consider emotions.

NAVIGATING CONFLICT

What happens when someone feels their position is attacked? Well, most people will get defensive and stubborn. We don't like being told we're wrong because it's belittling. So, our natural reaction is to dig our heels in deeper and not back down, even if part of us knows the other argument has some merit. Being human means, we have pride and don't want to lose face. So, directly saying someone else is completely wrong serves no purpose other than hurting feelings and shutting down the discussion. It becomes a clash of egos instead of an exchange of ideas.

The minute the other person senses you think their view has no validity; the walls will go up instantly. They'll stop hearing your perspective because they want to retaliate and condemn you. Most people fail to understand that your likeability can increase in arguments. What is the secret? Well, you have to find common ground. Compromise becomes impossible when both sides are entrenched in that argument. A situation that started with differing opinions transforms into a defensive battle where nobody is listening with an open mind anymore. Instead of a resolution, we end up with further resentment and no progress toward understanding each other.

Caring about resolving things peacefully is the better approach. Don't frame it as an issue of right versus wrong from the get-go. Show that you're willing to see validity in multiple viewpoints, including the other person's, even if you still partly disagree. Make it clear that their opinion is valued and that you want to find a solution together, not antagonise them into submission. The art of doing so keeps things from becoming personal or emotionally heated.

See disagreement not as something to defeat but as a chance to learn different perspectives. Ask questions to draw out someone's reasoning without it seeming like an interrogation. Express where you're coming from without demanding that they change their mind. Look for common ground to build on rather than differences to argue over. Surprising to some, society does have more similarities than differences. Compromise becomes possible when both sides explain their take without attacking the other.

Frame the discussion around interests and priorities rather than facts since values and goals are more debatable. Instead of "You are a compulsive liar and here is what I think" try "I understand why you see it that way based on what's important to you. Here's where I'm coming from based on my experience." Have empathy for how life experiences could lead equally reasonable people to divergent conclusions. Avoid perceived attacks on a character by keeping the subject about opinions, not people.

If emotions start rising, acknowledge them without dismissing them. Saying, "I can tell this matters a lot to you," or "I'm sure we both want what's best," calms tension better than rigidly debating merit alone. Again, many people want sympathy in arguments; give it to them, and they will love you. Take breaks if progress stalls to let heads cool without resolution. Rushing never ends well if feelings are running high.

NAVIGATING CONFLICT

Above all, remember, we're humans—driven more by emotions than sheer rationality. How we think and respond is fiercely tied to how we feel. So, to have a real discussion instead of a defensive argument, leave egos at the door and show compassion for others' perspectives alongside your own. Differences have the potential to provide learning opportunities, but if we handle them with force, those same differences will divide us permanently. Resolutions becomes possible when emotions are in mind, not proof of being right.

Discussions are most interesting when different ideas are exchanged freely. Skilled conversationalists know how to embrace differing views while still avoiding divisions. The secret is to keep exchanges focused on opinions, not attacks on character.

When disagreements surface in dialogue, the first instinct of many is to defend their stance adamantly and convince others they're correct. However, wise speakers show enthusiasm to hear opposing views. They display openness to potentially rethinking positions, and this welcoming spirit sets a cooperative tone from the outset, where all feel safe sharing unpopular takes.

Rather than demanding agreement, such a conversationalist asks thoughtful questions to grasp others' reasoning without judgment better. Their priority is learning, not winning. Even if they are privately unconvinced afterward, they acknowledge public perspectives with appreciation, not counterarguments. Likewise, people magnets take care to separate ideas from individuals, avoiding even subtle hints that the other person is flawed for differing. Disagreement exists only over differing viewpoints, nothing more, nothing less. Your aim should be to preserve civility - the foundation of any constructive exchange.

Should tension inadvertently rise, you should act without reaction to immediately defuse anger. Validate all feelings expressed and steer dialogue toward resolution – if possible. Make it a habit of informally thanking those involved for contributing new insights before gently moving the conversation to upbeat topics. As a result, bitterness rarely lingers.

Defusing Conflict

Admitting faults, making jokes, and agreeing to disagree are peaceful methods a person can use to defuse a touchy situation before conflict ignites. One technique is acknowledging when you may have misspoken or been too pushy in asserting your viewpoints. Simply saying, "You know, now that I think about it," or "You have a point; I could have phrased that better," goes a very long way. Admitting small mistakes takes the wind out of arguments by showing flexibility. Admit **your** mistakes before the other person does; it will weaken their defence. If you disagree with the other person, you may be tempted to interrupt, but do not do this. Don't try to condemn them, either. Try to understand them. People relax their guard when they feel heard instead of perpetually on the attack. Understand: You must call attention to your mistakes before criticising anyone. It cultivates an environment that brings down the guard of even the most suspicious people.

Humour can relieve pressures, too, when discussions start heating up. If needed, try making a self-deprecating joke if something you said came out wrong. Or find something silly both of you have experienced to chuckle about together. Laughter has a way of breaking tension like nothing else. As long as any humour steers clear of put-downs or sarcasm toward the other, it brings fun back to the exchange without dimming the seriousness of the issue.

Again, remember to take a brief break if emotions run too high on either side. Separating for 10 minutes allows things to cool down organically without forced resolution. Returning with fresher minds often makes previous tension seem trivial. Absence strengthens patience, while presence risks harsh words being said in a way that can't be taken back. Remind yourself that differing opinions don't define someone's worth, and often both parties want the best solution. With positive intent affirmed, harsh judgments soften, and the willingness to find harmony renews.

If an agreement remains impossible after the earnest exchange, propose respectfully to agree to disagree—and possibly revisit the issue as either learns more. Civil outcomes become achievable when the focus shifts from who is right to maintaining dignity and rapport among everyone involved.

Conflict often arises because people seek agreement for their views more than truly understanding others. Want the best way to diffuse tensions? Well, just show them sincere empathy. Society will always long to feel acknowledged. Therefore, most people are drawn to those who accept different perspectives rather than trying to change their minds through force. Agreement feels good, yes, but even more so does being heard without judgment. It's true: "People like people who agree with them." Hearing our stances echoed back affirms our self-worth whether you want to admit it or not. Rarely do individuals hold solely correct views on everything; presuming so strains relationships. A better approach embraces plurality graciously without demanding full consensus, which seldom comes.

Similarly, people do not win friends through arguments – true friends anyways. Debates prioritise beating opposition over unity, making others defensive rather than receptive. And yet, disputes can still benefit everyone if we replace attacks with empathy—seeing why others think as they do based on personal experiences. Challenging views should stem from curiosity, not a combative gotcha spirit closing off alternate perspectives. Questioning pushes understanding only when paired with active listening, not confrontation.

So, to defuse conflicts before they erupt, consider removing yourself from the conversation or changing the subject. Again, stepping away lets tensions ease without forcing immediate answers. Discussing lighter topics allows stressful ones to return when relationships are strong enough to handle differing takes. Forcing resolutions serves nobody.

Owning errors strengthens trust far beyond hollow denials or excuses that ring insincere. Saying, "You're correct; I misspoke,"

NAVIGATING CONFLICT

demonstrates integrity over bruised pride and is more valuable in the long term for building rapport. Vulnerability can disarm and bring people together where rigidity only divides. Faults feel embarrassing, but honesty facilitates understanding much better than hidden failings that fester with resentment. Likewise, forgiveness will come freely when you admit your wrongdoings – acknowledging it with sincerity.

SURRENDER TO EGOTISM

Many years ago, I had the privilege of playing for my university lacrosse team for three years. The team was exceptional, with dedicated players who shared a passion for the sport. However, one aspect of my experience tarnished my enjoyment of the game—the captain, whom I'll refer to as Matt for the sake of this narrative.

Now, let me be clear: Matt was undeniably talented and possessed unparalleled agility on the field. I must give credit where it's due. His passion for lacrosse ran deep, propelling him to strive for excellence and push the boundaries of his abilities.

However, during our second year, Matt's ego began to overshadow his talent. Matt was appointed team captain after our previous leader's sudden departure, and his ego swelled with pride. Unfortunately, this newfound sense of authority led him to wield his influence, so he made decisions without consulting our team and grew increasingly distant from the rest of us. It was as if he believed himself superior to the rest of the players, which created a toxic dynamic for everyone. Matt's unprincipled characteristic—

an insatiable ego that knew no bounds—was exacerbated by his tendency to surround himself with sycophants who only served to inflate his ego further with false praise.

As a result, the team dynamic shifted, and my love for the sport faded. With each passing game, it became increasingly evident that his leadership led our team to destruction. Morale plummeted, tensions reached a boiling point, and the once-united team began to fracture. In a moment of reckoning, Matt was finally forced to confront the consequences of his actions when the team confronted him about his behaviour. It took him several months to truly realise the gravity of his mistake. Still, to his credit, he eventually apologised to the team and vowed to change his ways—a promise he later succeeded in keeping.

As the third year of our university lacrosse journey ended, Matt and I stood on the sidelines, watching proudly as our teammates celebrated a hard-fought victory. Matt now understood that true leadership was not about power or authority but about uplifting others and bringing out the best in those around you. Indeed, the lesson from Matt's journey is timeless: remain humble despite successes, for humility truly defines a leader.

Let's be honest. When we talk to others, it's easy to get caught up in making ourselves look good while putting others down, but ego holds no credentials. If you want to win friends and strengthen those relationships, it's best to park your ego somewhere else. The goal should be to listen to and understand the other person, not just wait for your next chance to talk about yourself. Stay focused on them with your full attention. Be curious without judgment. You'll learn so much more, and people will feel heard. They'll be more likely to become transparent when there's no agenda other than connecting. Conversations are a chance to create community rather than drive people apart.

Now, let's imagine Ellis and Alivia are having a conversation over brunch. We'll see examples of how their egos can get in the way and damage the discussion. Then, you will discover how it is improved with ego absent.

Ellis has just finished telling Alivia about a recent holiday they took. Before she is even done with her story, Alivia interrupts. "Oh yeah, that sounds nice. But tell me about last year's holiday—it was way better!" Alivia then launches into a long story about all their activities on their trip, not letting Ellis get a word in. This is ego on Alivia's part. She fails to listen and wants to dominate the story to make her experience seem superior. It's unfair and frustrating.

You may think this is a rarity, but we all know people like this. What's truly remarkable is that some of them hold prominent positions. Egotistical individuals are solely focused on themselves, they often neglect the concerns of others. Sometimes, the ego in a conversation comes from just one person; it is often catastrophic if both parties involved have egos.

Here's another example, Sophia brags about a new promotion they got at work. "I'm now in charge of the whole department. It's a huge responsibility, but I'm up for it." Jack replies, "That's great and all, but haven't you heard? I'm looking to become the Vice

SURRENDER TO EGOTISM

President of the whole company in a few years. Being in charge of a department is small compared to my opportunity." Jack has discussed his own (possible) future success instead of celebrating Sophia's professional achievement.

Let's say Dylan tells Luke that he has started learning French in their free time. Luke replies, "Hmm, French is overrated if you ask me. If you want to challenge yourself, try learning Mandarin. That is so much harder, but it would look great on your resume." Again, Luke fails to listen or be supportive; they instead insert their own opinion to imply that their language choice would be better. Do not doubt that there are people in this world who project egos as heavy as this; it happens more than you might think.

Let's imagine the same conversation scenario without ego getting in the way. After Ellis shares about their holiday, Alivia says, "Wow, it sounds like you had an enjoyable trip! I'm glad we were able to get away and enjoy yourself. What was your favourite part of the trip?" Ellis can finish telling their story without being interrupted. When it's Alivia's turn, they focus on asking questions rather than launching into their own holiday experience.

When Sophia discusses their work promotion, Jack responds, "Congrats! It's great that your hard work has been recognised. What will your new role entail, and how do you feel about the increased responsibilities?" Jack makes the conversation about her accomplishments rather than himself. And when Dylan mentions learning French, Luke says, "That's so cool you're taking up a new language. French must be interesting to study; are you enjoying the process?" Luke is now supportive rather than critical.

With ego out of the picture, the discussions focus on celebrating the other person rather than competition or one-upmanship. Both individuals feel their contributions have value. That is the power of letting the other person have the spotlight. Socialising without ego is perfectly possible, and the rewards will pay in dividends.

Resolutions for Removing Ego

You must remove your ego to become a people magnet, win friends, perfect dialogue and learn the art of likability. Here are a few techniques you can use right away to keep any pride from overshadowing your potential.

- **Be a good listener:** Many believe this is common sense, yet very few apply it. As they say, God gave us two ears and one mouth for a reason. So, focus wholly on what they're sharing without thinking about how you'll respond. Don't interrupt or daydream. Hear them out.

- **Ask probing questions:** Getting the other person to open up takes effort. Rather than closed questions with a yes or no, use inquiries that delve deeper, like "What was that experience like for you?" or "How did you feel?". Respond thoughtfully to their answers to show your presence.

- **Leave room for others to contribute:** Dominating discussions and desiring the limelight feeds our egos but exhaust everyone else. Look for natural breaks in conversations to politely cede the floor back to the other speaker. Show you value what they bring to the table.

- **Validate others' feelings and experiences:** Instead of being quick to one-up or claim you've been through worse, recognise their emotions as real and important as yours. Saying things like, "It makes total sense that it bothers you," are humble stances that foster trust.

- **Highlight common ground:** Noting a point of connection ("I had a similar experience last month, too") brings people together in fellowship versus acts that split hairs over distinctions. We all have more likeness than unlikeness if we seek it with good faith.

- **Lose the comparison game:** Drop thoughts like "My situation is tougher" or "I personally feel I do that better than you." Outside of occasional healthy jokes between friends, competitive one-upping only pushes people away.

- **Say "we" to involve others:** When discussing shared goals or group activities, utilise plural terms that signify teamwork over sole credit-taking. "We made such progress on this project together" instead of "I accomplished much progress on this project."

- **Be complimentary, not braggadocious:** Look for sincere, credible praise about others that feels meaningfully reflective rather than empty flattery to inflate your character. Be specific, not generic.

- **Control impulses to interrupt:** Before butting in, consciously ask yourself: Does what I want to say improve the current discussion, or is it just a sidebar serving my ego? If the latter, be patient.

Remember, true humility isn't thinking less of yourself but of yourself less. Relationships blossom without hindrance when your focus shifts to others and ordinary discussions elevate into profound exchanges. Humility is simply considering someone else more significant than you, which leads to the sweet fruit of selflessness in all our communications.

So, you now have practical steps to try out. Be fully present, ask thoughtful questions, validate feelings, and amplify common ground through "we" language. Step back from competition to let others dominate the conversation. These techniques will gradually remove ego from your professional or personal conversations.

VULNERABILTY IS A MUST

Have you ever clicked with someone immediately, like you've known them your whole life even though you just met? Chances are, there was some vulnerability involved. Or have you struggled to connect with others, no matter how long you've known them? That's often because neither of you lets your guard down. The truth is that being willing to show your weaknesses selectively is crucial for relationships.

Your vulnerability is an asset. So, share things you're not proud of or things you regret. It's admitting when we're scared, confused, or damaged in some way instead of keeping up an image of having it all together. We put down our guard and give others a glimpse at the imperfect person underneath. I admit, this does take courage because it leaves us open to being hurt but also clears the way for intimacy.

Society is naturally drawn to others who seem genuine. We can smell inauthenticity a mile away. By putting on a mask or pretending always to be happy, strong, and in control, we avoid any meaningful connections. People can't get close if they don't know the real you—only the character you portray. Vulnerability is how we trust others enough to let our guard down, allowing them to trust and confide in us, too. It's a powerful sign of bravery.

Sharing our vulnerabilities helps people understand us beyond surface-level small talk. When we're willing to be emotionally honest, it provides invaluable context for those in our lives. They see what shaped us into who we are today rather than just the finished product. Your story is your testimony. One that draws people to support us since they now comprehend us as whole individuals instead of vague acquaintances.

Of course, vulnerability requires tact and discretion. We don't want to traumatise people or dump too many heavy issues onto new friends. But finding the courage to slowly share a few soft spots over time as trust develops is so valuable. Once your relationships have solidified, telling your new friend that you grew up in a toxic family, you struggled with gambling, or you regret cheating on your spouse may not be surprising information. However, telling this exact information initially would question your character.

It can be scary to believe people won't reject or use your weaknesses against you, so use your ability to discern others. Those relationships will remain idle chatter if we never take that chance. Our support systems stay shallow where transparency could have deepened them significantly.

So yes, vulnerability is necessary, but there is also such a thing as revealing too much too fast before a friendship has had time to develop. Dumping a ton of personal information on someone we barely know can easily backfire and do more harm than good. So, starting small with light vulnerability is paramount as we get to know a new person and test the waters of trust.

One strategy is to begin by sharing safe topics that don't immediately expose our deepest insecurities or traumas. Simple things like values or observations about our day are low-risk ways to open up. Comments like, "I really get into hiking on weekends" or "Treating others with kindness is important to me." Avoid laying everything on the line emotionally. They give the other person a taste of who you are without overwhelming them.

Another approach is to qualify vulnerability by remarking that it's something you haven't discussed much before. "I don't often share this, but..." or "You're one of the few people I've talked about my experience with..." frames a disclosure as a special sign of budding trust rather than a hardcore information dump. It seems less pressure and feels more like an honour for the other person to receive this new information about you at that early stage.

Also, be cautious of immediately unloading past problems loaded with emotional baggage onto acquaintances. We understand previous struggles have likely shaped who we are, but spewing graphic details of traumas can scare people off prematurely before they've committed to really getting to know us. It's okay to allude to the fact that life hasn't always been easy or that you've faced adversity without belabouring the gruesome details upfront.

So, you must pay close attention to cues that the other person seems uncomfortable with or is at a loss for how to respond.

Respect signs that they may need more time to consume all the information. A good rule is that if you've said something intimate and it's met with a long silence, you've likely crossed a line at that stage in the friendship.

Test the waters gradually over many low-stakes interactions. Share one small thing, then see how they respond before divulging more. Build comfort and understanding incrementally rather than opening the vault all at once. Being attuned to relationship growth in this observant manner creates appropriate disclosure paces that someone new is ready to receive. Also, ask questions to show interest in getting to know others better during this initial phase.

Ask innocuous things like what neighbourhood they live in, how long they've worked at their current job or their favourite movie. Equal give-and-take is needed. Avoid sharing personal problems, dark secrets, or excessive trauma histories that could overwhelm someone you barely know.

My advice is simple: keep early vulnerability positive or strengths focused. Mentioning past accomplishments or general world views establishes openness without bumming the other person out right away. Once comfort emerges after consistent meetups, then sensitive topics become healthier and better-received options to bring up. Finding the perfect balance will enhance your influence in social circles. Remember, it's also fine to talk about the challenges or difficulties that made you the resilient person you are today. For example, learning from failed relationships or how being bullied as a youth shaped your compassion for others. Reciprocation is important, too. So, after hearing about someone's adventure backpacking in Europe, share how you'd love to hike more if work permitted it.

When bringing up major issues, prime the discussion by expressing how much the relationship means to you and how this person's good qualities inspire sharing private struggles. For example, "Our friendship has helped me grow so much. I can trust you with this difficult part of my story." "You've supported me so much that I want to share my struggle with depression these last few years." "Being this open does not come easy for me, but I trust you with this, like my family's experience with addiction."

Major vulnerable topics could include delicate family secrets, private mental health battles, traumatic past experiences, deep insecurities, or things never told to many others before. In return, actively listen with empathy. Also, ask thoughtful questions to understand their perspective, avoid criticism or one-upmanship, express genuine care, and sincerely thank them for confiding in you. By layering disclosure at thoughtful paces, vulnerability can bring people closer while respecting individual limits. Both parties gain from the courage of an honest connection.

Vulnerability Holds Risk

As the old saying goes, nothing ventured, nothing gained. And it's true when it comes to forming close bonds with others—there's simply no reward without first taking on some risk. If we never open our hearts in conversations or welcome discomfort, how can we ever really know someone or be known in return? Those deep connections require vulnerability, and with vulnerability comes a chance of hurt. But avoiding risk also guarantees loneliness, so we must choose to roll the dice and pray for the best.

We inevitably expose ourselves to harm when we expose our secrets or weaknesses. We give others potential leverage over our feelings and self-worth. Our pride might get bruised if they react poorly to what is revealed or even use it against us later in an argument. We could feel rejected if they don't understand or don't reciprocate our feelings. There is a risk the relationship fails, with disastrous results from misplaced confidence.

Nevertheless, if we hide behind emotional armour and polite small talk, it protects us from none of life's uncertainties. There is no point in having acquaintances who barely know our hearts – it will leave us depressed and unfulfilled. By shutting down vulnerability in self-defence, we end up just as lonely, with fewer chances to create strong bonds. The ironically safer route society trains us to take often feels far lonelier.

Closing ourselves off from opportunities to let others truly know and support us comes at an isolation price too heavy for most. There are no guarantees of security in opening up, but gradually taking leaps of faith at least provides a shot at meaningful results.

Being vulnerable doesn't condemn our entire well-being to someone else's whims. We develop resilience through practising transparency. Not every friend warrants those deep glimpses right

VULNERABILITY IS A MUST

away. We learn which people elevate our lives versus those who derail our self-worth. Plus, the people worth keeping around long-term will usually rise to meet our trust and understanding. Nobody's perfect. Relationships take work from both sides, but people magnets aim to nurture what's born of another's bravery.

MASTERY OF SMALL TALK

Engaging in polite small talk feels like a social obligation we must endure. Exchanging superficial pleasantries about the weather or weekend plans seems inevitable. Yet this ritualistic chitchat often leaves us unfulfilled and wanting a more meaningful connection. Small talk feels so unsatisfying because it lacks authenticity. We share statements like "Wow! It's a nice day today" as decorative conversation fillers, not to convey any real insight or interest. The topic is just a placeholder until a more substantial subject emerges organically. However, relying on vague banalities hinders authentic relationships.

While some introverts avoid small talk to escape draining social rituals, even extroverts yearn for depth. Curious people want exchanges where we learn each other's perspectives, values, and dreams. The solution that takes interactions to a level beyond trite observations will be addressed shortly.

First, simply being mindful about sharing meaningful ideas rather than defaulting to dull chatter can shift energy. If you catch yourself starting with the inevitable "How are you?" try substituting a sincere "What's inspiring you lately?" Feel free to re-word this formally or informally.

Second, conversations should focus on emotional experiences and ideas, not just facts and events. Ask creative questions to uncover how people think and see the world. Reflect on the feelings behind their stories.

Third, open up about your own life on a slightly deeper level. Be vulnerable about your passions, struggles, and lessons learned. People are more willing to open up and be vulnerable when they feel safe and understood. Modelling authentic self-disclosure inspires it in others. Small talk has its time and place for smoothing social interactions. But great conversations thrive on genuineness and insight. So, when we engage without hiding behind platitudes, human connections will flourish.

Moving past mundane small talk to substantive conversation requires intention and skill. One effective strategy is to start exchanges based on common interests rather than superficial observations. Clever opening lines may impress, but simple vulnerability builds trust.

Empty chatter about benign topics like the weather fills awkward silences between strangers and acquaintances. "Hot enough for you?" "Some storm last night, huh?" This lacks depth. Your likability increases when people know more about you, which is often revealed through your vulnerability as small talk alone will never achieve this.

We must push past the conditioned tendency toward banalities to foster authentic relationships. An organic transition is sometimes presented through laughter at a shared observation or a serendipitous compliment: "That baking smells amazing!" This can lead to swapping recipes or cooking tips.

Other times, you can proactively guide the discussion to the more interesting ground by asking open-ended questions or sharing personal passions. If you suspect common interests, pivot from the forgettable small talk. For instance, at a school social, rather than saying "Good to see you!" to fellow parents, discuss your kids' grade levels, teachers, and after-school activities. Or, with colleagues you know love hiking on the weekends, transition quickly into comparing favourite trails instead of bland weather remarks.

Look for visual clues like clothing, jewellery, or tattoos indicating hobbies and ask about them. If someone is carrying a camera, ask if photography is a passion. The goal is to jump to subjects that excite you both. Talking about the other person's interests should benefit all parties involved.

Don't worry about appearing clever. A little vulnerability and honesty work magic. For example, "I always struggle when dealing with small talk, but I'm interested in photography. What got you into it?" This openness and directness are relieving. Small talk may be unavoidable, but it need not dominate.

Break the ice with personal sharing. Once you've broken the ice, share parallel experiences to deepen rapport.

I spoke with a passenger on a plane from London, Heathrow to Dallas, Texas. I was open about my hesitations about flying. "I'm a nervous flier, so take-offs make me anxious. What about you?" This admission of vulnerability surprised my reserved seatmate, but he confided that flying wasn't their favourite either, though he had improved over the years.

That moment of realising we shared this sweet spot of common experience—anxiety around flying but doing it anyway—created an immediate bond. We swapped strategies for managing fears and favourite distractions during flights. The transparency allowed a momentary friendship to form through mutual understanding.

As we prepared to land, my new friend asked for my contact information, saying, "We should stay in touch." The request took me aback, but I gladly exchanged numbers.

Over the following weeks, we messaged each other frequently, sharing stories from our lives and journeys. It turned out we only lived about 45 minutes apart. We arranged to meet for coffee and quickly realised we had become good friends.

Our families also bonded well. Ten years have passed since that initial plane ride and we have supported each other through challenges and celebrated many happy times together. Family vacations became joint affairs; our children are like an extended family; they call me "Uncle," and my kids see him as a mentor.

It is truly amazing to reflect on how opening up to one stranger on a plane led to such a meaningful friendship. That initial act of vulnerability taught me to take social risks. Breaking out of my shell allowed a caring relationship to develop, bringing so much joy and support. I'm grateful fate placed us side by side that day, giving me a lifelong friend I might otherwise have missed out on.

Had I commented on generic aspects of travel, that opportunity for connection would have been lost. Being open made the difference. Of course, you must gauge appropriate levels of disclosure depending on the situation. But usually, we do underestimate how receptivity to candour facilitates relationships.

Once you've broken the ice with transparency, you can build on that foundation of trust by linking questions to establish shared interests or experiences. For instance, after bonding over our airport anxieties, my seatmate and I discovered we were both teachers headed to a similar conference in different states. That led naturally to more teaching stories and perspectives. That is the power of one conversation.

The conversation flowed effortlessly once inhibitions were lowered. Given the established rapport, we felt invested in learning about each other's lives and views. I learned fascinating insights from someone I might never have exchanged more than pleasantries with. So, give this a try next time you want to connect past surface niceties. Be brave in sharing something real, and see how it unlocks reciprocal authenticity in others - you have more in common than you know.

Make it a habit of following up with broader openers once you uncover commonalities. For instance, if you learn the person enjoys hiking as much as you do, ask where they like to hike locally – it may present you with an opportunity to join them on their next hike. Or, if they mention having kids, you can inquire about their ages and activities.

I must admit, building confidence often means taking the plunge and just doing it. Some lessons are best learned through taking a leap of faith and seeing where it leads. My own confidence grew significantly when I started attending social events in my area, which allowed me to meet a diverse range of people.

Imagine this scenario: You live in Glasgow, Scotland, and have identified a niche interest—say, tennis. A quick search on Facebook, TikTok or Instagram could help you find local groups that meet weekly or monthly, providing the perfect opportunity to connect with like-minded individuals. Engaging in these activities will boost your confidence.

Here are some examples of effective sequencing:

- "What do you enjoy doing on weekends?"

- "You said you love live music; what local bands specifically?"

- "Ah, a fellow music fan! What instruments do you play?"

Or, if you have both moved to the area:

- "How long have you lived here?"

- "Just a few months? How has the adjustment been?"

- "I feel out of place too. What are your favourite discoveries?"

Tailoring questions to evolving commonalities carries the dialogue. It ensures you don't just burden people with getting-to-know-you small talk, which they've answered countless times. This fluid questioning also takes the pressure off needing to be endlessly witty. The focus lands on the other person rather than your performance. Let their responses guide you rather than following a script. Try building on what you have in common to take the conversation to rich places.

Topics to Explore if Conversation Stalls

Conversations hit a lull sometimes. So, steering the discussion toward people's families, occupations, hobbies, and future goals breathes new life into the exchange. These fundamental areas provide windows into what shapes individuals and brings meaning to their lives. Even small talk can lead to big insights if redirected toward these rich topics. Family relationships and upbringing often shape people's values and worldviews. Asking thoughtful questions about family provides understanding, even if your own differs.

"Where did you grow up?" opens the door to exchanging perspectives on regional cultures. "What was it like having X siblings?" reveals how family size affects social dynamics. "How did your parents encourage your talents as a kid?" uncovers influential parenting styles. Follow up with parallel experiences.

Discussing occupations also has layers of fulfilment beyond just stating job titles. Explore what drew them to their field—challenges they navigated, milestones, and setbacks they faced. Ask educators why they teach and artists what inspires them. Recognition of career passions satisfies our shared desire to be understood. And we all love to be understood.

Their hobbies and interests may often be gold mines for tales and shared experiences. For example, fellow dog owners might swap stories about neighbourhood pooches, or amateur photographers might trade technique tips. Identify these times of commonality.

Plans and dreams reveal people's hopes and values. Is a career change on the horizon? Where do they wish to travel? What's on their bucket list? Exploring goals helps you appreciate what matters most to someone. Sometimes, conversation requires gently guiding it to these uplifting places.

Making someone feel comfortable sharing about themselves requires thoughtful listening and reinforcement. It means implementing supportive language and showing a genuine interest, so you create an environment where others feel safe.

Inviting disclosure from even reserved individuals is an art that begins with making them feel heard and respected. Make appropriate eye contact and give your full attention when they speak. In a group, pay attention to everyone; do not exclude anyone. Verbal affirmations like "I see" and "That's so interesting" convey that you are wholly engaged.

Draw out more details and feelings. "What was that experience like for you?" or "How did that make you feel?" shows your eagerness to gain their perspective. Remember, this can be worded in a formal or informal way.

Paraphrase what you hear: "It sounds like that was a difficult transition for you." Also, share your own relevant experiences to demonstrate empathy. "When I went through something similar, I also felt overwhelmed." This reciprocity models openness. Occasionally, summarise the conversation to highlight important revelations. "So, it seems like after college, you found your creative path once you discovered photography." The truth is many people do this subconsciously. Nevertheless, this strategy should be used with informal language, too.

When someone becomes more transparent, affirm how much you appreciate their openness. Few things are more important than expressing your gratitude. Also, take care not to dominate any conversation with too many interjections. Make sure ample space remains for them to share comfortably. Exclusive attention to the person speaking is paramount. Those who talk excessively often don't want your advice. Instead, they desire a sympathetic listener to whom they can unload information. That is what we all desire. Your role is primarily encouraging them rather than asserting your own perspectives.

You'll learn, through experience, when to probe deeper and when to listen. When people feel accepted without judgment, walls naturally lower and you have the potential to lower the guards of the most stubborn individuals. Master this, and you will become influential in conversations.

ESTABLISH A GOOD NAME

Small talk does play a role when you first meet someone new. When we talk about the inevitable topics, it does help break the ice and makes people feel comfortable. There's nothing wrong with small talk. It's a nice way to start a conversation. However, you must learn to master it by developing it.

Yes, small talk is great for passing the time or filling an awkward silence, but it never tells much about another person. Discussing superficial topics only takes you so far before the conversation feels empty and repetitive. The problem with depending solely on small talk is that it becomes predictable and fails to satisfy our need for sincere interaction and intimacy with others. Remember, people don't just want superficial relationships; we all crave genuine bonds where we feel truly known and understood by someone else. Small talk alone does not offer much. So, how do you transition a conversation from idle pleasantries into more significant territory?

You've heard a lot about this throughout this book. ***Ask open-ended questions.*** These require more than a simple yes, no, or a one-worded response. Instead of "How was your weekend?" which often elicits "Good, thanks," try asking something like "What did you enjoy most about your weekend and why?" Now, the person has to think about their answer and share more personal details and perspectives. You'll learn more about their personalities through their responses. Here is another word of advice: ensure you carry these questions with confidence. Be passionate when you ask others, it will motivate them to respond receptively.

Another tip is to share something more meaningful about yourself and invite the other person to reciprocate. For instance, instead of the standard "What do you do for work?" you could say, "I just switched to a new role where I get to be more creative—it's great but also a big adjustment. What do you find most rewarding about your job?" Now, you've revealed something more personal about your lives while opening the door for others to discuss what matters to them in their careers.

You should also watch for opportunities to steer the conversation toward topics the other person is passionate about. Social media is now a powerful application that allows anyone to find out the interests of others in a matter of seconds. You will find everything you need to know in one search, one click. Find out what their interests are and start a conversation around them. If you try to study their interests, it will grant you great results.

Furthermore, share your honest opinions with reason instead of just agreeing with whatever the other person says. Show your confidence and encourage them to do the same. You can even respectfully disagree without creating divisions, saying, "That's an interesting perspective. Personally, I do feel differently about XYZ because..." shows you're comfortable being authentic while letting them retain their views, too.

Don't be afraid of moments of silence, either. Resist the urge to jump in and re-start small talk if pauses occur immediately. Sometimes, the most meaningful insights come from periods of quiet reflection. See if the other person may be quietly mulling over something you discussed, and be open to listening if they feel inclined to share deeper thoughts.

Express genuine care and follow up on previous discussions instead of letting conversations fade away and restarting from scratch each time. For example, ask about a trip they mentioned last week or how their presentation went for their job interview. Recall little personal details from prior chats to say, "How did settling into the new house go?"

Show your character. They must get a good idea of who you are. So, when talking to others, share sentimental elements of your personality, motivations, and outlooks. Are you honest and moral? Hard-working or easy-going? Thoughtful or carefree? Be willing to demonstrate your true character. So, if integrity is important to you, don't just say it; show it by keeping your word. Compliment others sincerely. Humbly admit if you're wrong rather than stubbornly insisting your view is solely right. Those subtle glimpses of your character will make others want to learn more about you.

ESTABLISH A GOOD NAME

Your motivations drive who you are just as much as your character. Make sure to convey what sparks your passion and fire in life. Maybe it's your family, career goals, hobbies, or dreams for the future. For instance, don't just say you love your job; explain what excites you about helping others through your line of work. Understanding someone's motivations enables you to cheer them on and find common ground if your purposes align.

All your unique experiences shape your perspective, so it's worth sharing sometimes. How you view certain topics or situations will differ greatly from others. Provide insights into how your perspective has formed over time. For example, if travel has expanded your outlook, discuss a moment from a past trip that shifted how you see other cultures now. Your personality also plays a role. You may tend to see the glass half full due to your generally optimistic nature. Letting your perspective shine gives others a renewed appreciation for their viewpoint and helps them better understand how you think about life circumstances.

Not everyone feels comfortable disclosing personal details. Therefore, use personal examples and stories to bring your outlook alive. So, instead of flatly saying, "I'm motivated by helping others," maybe you could share, "I'll never forget when I volunteered at the soup kitchen on Easter —there was this one lady who had lost everything in a house fire but was still so grateful to have a warm meal. Her spirit stuck with me and that is why I pursued this career path." Showing your true self through real-life vignettes cements you as a sincere, rounded individual.

If moments arise where your traits relate directly to the conversation topic, seizing those opportunities to illustrate yourself makes perfect sense. Don't force an "all about me" performance or overshadow what others share. Instead, look for occasional and natural ways to subtly reveal your qualities by building on discussion points everyone can stay engaged in. The key is moderation: aim for others to learn bits about you here and there rather than bombarding them with "me, me, me!"

Making true friends as adults can be hard since we're all so busy with other responsibilities. Some have children. Some have partners. Some are family battles. And yet, the good news is that it is possible - it just takes being intentional with others.

People love it when you show genuine interest in learning who they truly are rather than just having a conversation. People love those who talk about them. We all have unique stories—funny adventures, challenges, and lessons learned. So, share them boldly and enhance your influence.

Stories paint vibrant pictures that facts and superficial chat alone can't achieve. They help friends feel truly seen and known by one another. So maybe you can bond while laughing together about the time a prank went wrong in high school or draw strength from discussing a struggle one of you recently overcame.

Of course, close friendships take effort and commitment to develop and maintain over the years. That is why checking in, being supportive through life stages, and making time for each other despite busy schedules will keep the bond strong. So, next time you meet someone new with potential, see them as more than a fleeting interaction; see them as a future friend.

The consensus is that we should extend kindness and respect to all individuals, irrespective of our differences. And yet, our brains are often wired to feel a closer bond with those who remind us of ourselves. This makes us more likely to offer help to others just like us instead of strangers who are dissimilar - these instincts could create divisions.

Many studies have found that we instinctively favour those of a similar race, religion, or country over outsiders when allocating resources or making charitable donations (Everett et al., 2015). This in-group preference seems to stem from evolutionary instincts that favour those closest to us genetically. That is why consciously focusing on our shared humanity remains important regardless of surface differences. Find points where your lives connect, no matter how trivial they may seem. These human tendencies are enlightening, but we should not discount acts of altruism shown to those different from us. Unconscious biases tend to recede, so we must expose ourselves to diversification.

Connection Stories

When you meet someone new, share quick stories about yourself. Not all stories are created equal; some will engage the listener, while others may fall flat or even turn them off. Let's examine examples of what makes for a good connection story versus a bad one. A good connection story will draw the listener in by painting a vivid picture they can easily visualise and relate to. For instance, say you enjoy camping and meet someone who likes the outdoors. You could share:

"Just last summer, some mates and I ended up on a weekend backpacking trip in the mountains. On the first night, a huge rainstorm hit, and our little tent started leaking like crazy. We had to bail out all our gear in the dark just to stay dry! Eventually, the downpour let up, and we found a spot to string up a tarp for shelter. The forest was soaked by morning, but the sunrise peaking over the treetops made up for the late-night scare. Nights like that are what camping memories are all about, you know?"

That short anecdote sets a scene anyone can picture vividly through descriptive details. The relatable element of unexpected weather challenges, paired with ultimately making the best of it, helps the listener empathise rather than feel the distance. They may now think about inviting you along to their next outdoor trip since your story left them wanting more.

In contrast, a bad connection story will fail to paint a clear scene or relate on a personal level, and it risks disconnecting the listener. An example could be: "So, last weekend, I went with some people to do an outdoor thing. It rained a lot one night, and we had to move stuff around outside in the dark. But then it got better, and the scenery was nice at sunrise. Outdoor adventures, am I right?"

ESTABLISH A GOOD NAME

This bare-bones, low-effort retelling provides little imagery or context for why the listener should care. Without vivid clues about who was involved, where it happened, and tangible details that paint an experience they can feel part of vicariously, it falls flat. Unfortunately, it ends up as more of an obligatory statement than an engaging window into someone's world worth learning more about. Good stories illustrate something meaningful about the storyteller's character, priorities, or sense of humour. For instance, you may share:

"I'll never forget the family camping trip to Lake Tahoe when I was 10. My little brother fell into the lake and started panicking; as the oldest, I had to jump in fully clothed to pull him out. We were both soaked and cold, but my mom's proud smile as we sat by the fire made it all worth it. I still love those feeling-like-a-hero moments protecting my siblings." This taps into relatable family dynamics during formative years to give insight into someone as caring and responsible without directly stating, "I'm caring!" Bad stories may boast empty claims like "I'm brave" without showing their true colours in an engaging story.

Keeping stories positive or finding the lesson without trashing others is also best. Complaining turns people off. But a story can still have a vulnerability, like:

"Starting my property business was scary. I put everything into it, but some months were touch-and-go if I'd make rent. One client, who gave me a chance when I felt doubtful, changed everything. I'll never forget their support; I try to pay kindness forward in my work today whenever possible." This shows grit and gratitude through a low moment. Bad stories elicit negative emotions without providing redemptive insights for the listener.

OTHERS BEFORE ME

People are, above all, interested in themselves, so you must understand people to strive socially and increase likability. If you talk to people about themselves, they will show enormous interest. And I cannot stress this enough: your objective is to put ourselves in someone else's shoes. Try to see the world through their experiences briefly before offering counterarguments. Ask open-ended questions to draw them out so you can gain more insight into what's important to them.

Understanding others doesn't require agreeing with them on everything. But it does require empathy—the ability to appreciate another's viewpoint even if you don't share it fully. And empathy is a big part of bringing people together. When we sincerely try to comprehend the actions of others, it helps them feel heard and respected in return.

Seek first to understand and prevent unintentional conflicts. Friction often arises from making assumptions without knowing all the facts, so ask for clarity and never assume. Not everything needs to be a debate; sometimes, we can gain insight through attentive listening. So, you must be willing to learn instead of always needing to be an expert. This will require flexibility instead of rigidity when our own views are challenged. Gaining new perspectives is how we grow in wisdom. And making connections by truly listening to what's meaningful for another person creates closer bonds between all kinds of people.

The Likability Factor

We all want people to like us. So, to cultivate social relationships, we must genuinely be likeable to others. Most people are primarily focused on themselves—what interests them, what affects them directly, and what benefits their situation the most.

We all have a certain level of self-interest driving our thoughts and actions. It's only natural to be more concerned with issues that impact us personally than with things far removed. And we're naturally inclined to form stronger bonds with those who see things similarly to how we view the world. So, when talking with others next time, it's good to remember that their priorities are significantly shaped by self-interest like all of ours are.

This is why taking the time to understand another person's perspective makes a difference in how much they'll like engaging with you. Most people neglect the basic principle of showing genuine interest because they cannot see the consequences of not applying it. Showing you tried seeing an issue from their standpoint shows your care about what matters to them. People feel respected. People feel valued. And people feel noticed. That interest people show in us is a powerful motivator to do good—and for those with a twisted mind, to do bad. So, to make others feel important, we first need to believe they *are*.

Social media is now a powerful application that allows users to find out the interests of others in a matter of seconds. Your aim should be to find out their interests and start a conversation around them. If you try to study their interests, it will grant you great results.

As I journeyed back home to London from a business event in Bristol, I decided to pass the time by tuning in to a relational podcast. The episode delved into the power of common interests and the trajectory of conversations centred around them. The host shared a compelling story about his friends, Reanna and Jack, who shared a mutual love for running despite residing in different towns. Given the brevity of the podcast, I'll summarise the key points.

Week after week, Reanna and Jack faithfully attended their respective run clubs. Their passion united them for pounding the pavement and pushing their limits on the open road. During one of these club runs, their paths serendipitously crossed, igniting a lively connection that served as the perfect icebreaker. As they exchanged stories of past races and training triumphs, they engaged in a spirited conversation, which led to eagerly exchanging tips to improve their performance on the road.

Running served as their shared interest. Therefore, their attention increased when the topic of running was mentioned. The podcast also touched upon the reality that not all interests may align and how interacting with individuals who hold opposing interests can lead to tiresome exchanges.

The key takeaway from the podcast was clear: if someone's interest does not resonate with you, the conversation may serve a purpose for only a limited time. However, even if the topic may not initially pique your interest, engaging with genuine curiosity can benefit both parties. The host concluded this segment of the podcast with this gentle reminder: conversations become truly enriching when the person expressing their interest **and** the one receiving the attention benefit from them.

People are much less likely to feel a strong bond with those who only ever speak about themselves. Coming across that way signals that you view others mainly as an audience rather than as complex individuals deserving respect. It also shows you're self-absorbed, which damages how much someone genuinely likes you.

The Art of Empathy

Showing empathy is great. The ability to understand someone from their perspective rather than just our own, opens doors for increased likability. People are naturally more invested in conversations that reference them.

Practising empathy begins with attentive listening without assumptions. We must resist the urge to form premature judgments and instead truly hear what others say on their own terms first. Make appropriate eye contact, put away distractions and ask clarifying questions respectfully. Give your full attention without planning rebuttals so the speaker feels understood.

Incorporate details from the other person's life into your conversation whenever feasible. For example, saying something like "Considering your situation with young children, I can get the challenges you're facing" personalises the interaction and will also demonstrate an attempt to empathise with their perspective. We all prefer to discuss views through our unique circumstances rather than abstract opinions alone. Tailoring interactions to who the other person is can build instant rapport.

Try restating their perspective in your own words and check for accuracy. You will show them you've comprehended where they're coming from. Saying something like "If I understand correctly, your main concern is…" acknowledges complex reasons and informs all stances. Rarely do absolute rights or wrongs exist.

Share related details from your own life, too, when relevant, so discussions stay balanced. Ask how a situation makes them feel on top of just facts alone. Emotions provide keys to empathising at soul levels beyond surface narratives. Inviting disclosure creates atmospheric intimacy where all voices matter versus combative debates. Admitting preconceived biases and keeping an open mind builds equity where people feel heard, not judged.

Complexities require seeing multiple realities coexist versus antagonistic right or wrong stances that divide.

Make it a habit of directing discussions toward mutual learning. Note areas for personal growth just as much as points demanding agreement. Admit flaws graciously when warranted, rather than denying them, which strains goodwill. Remember to take breaks if overstimulation hinders true empathy. Separating and then regrouping with a fresh perspective prevents frustrations.

At its heart, empathy does make people feel motivated and understood. So, remember, people are, above all else, interested in themselves, so invest time in knowing them sincerely and watch yourself strive socially.

KEEP YOUR HANDS CLEAN

We've all been there—getting together with friends or coworkers and slipping into idle gossip. It can be easy to start making judgments and spreading rumours without realising it. But as fun as gossip may seem in the moment, it rarely leads anywhere good and often does real harm.

On the surface, gossip might seem like a harmless way to bond with others or get things off our chests – and sometimes it fulfils us. But underneath, it's rarely as innocent as it appears. When we start criticising people behind their backs, making assumptions about their motives, or spreading private details they've shared in confidence, we risk hurting their reputation and our own. Even if our intentions aren't malicious, the effects can still damage trust and cause pain for those on the receiving end.

Passing casual judgments is also problematic because it's human nature to paint a one-sided, incomplete picture of someone based on limited information. We don't have the full context of another person's life experiences, relationships, emotions, or private challenges away from public view. We often form opinions about people without truly understanding their situation, yet the consequences can be catastrophic. Making declarations about who they are as a whole person often ends up being unfair.

The detrimental effects of gossip extend beyond just those talked about above. Indulging regularly in criticism fosters cynicism within ourselves and poisons relationships. It creates unhealthy social dynamics where people feel pressured to put others down to fit in or prove their loyalty. Many businesses have experienced the dire effects of gossip, resulting in a damaged reputation.

PepsiCo serves as an example of a company whose reputation was severely damaged by rumours, particularly involving their flagship product. The incident is often dubbed as the "Pepsi Syringe Scare."

In 1993, a man in Washington state claimed that he found a syringe in a can of Diet Pepsi. The alarming report quickly led to a flood of similar claims across the United States, with consumers alleging they discovered foreign objects, including syringes, in their cans of Pepsi products. The media extensively covered these reports, causing public panic and significant damage to PepsiCo's reputation.

As the scare grew, the FDA and PepsiCo took action by launching thorough investigations. PepsiCo even aired a video showing their production process to reassure the public that it was impossible for such contaminants to enter the cans during manufacturing. The video depicted the high-speed filling and sealing of cans, emphasising the stringent quality control measures in place.

Thankfully, the turning point came when surveillance footage from a convenience store caught a woman inserting a syringe into a can of Diet Pepsi, proving that at least some of the claims were fraudulent. The FDA eventually declared the scare a hoax, with no credible evidence to suggest that Pepsi products were tampered with during production and manufacturing phase.

Despite this vindication, the incident had already taken a toll. PepsiCo experienced decreased profits as they had to invest heavily in a robust public relations campaign to rebuild consumer trust. They ran full-page ads in major newspapers, created television spots, and leveraged media interviews to communicate the findings of their investigation and the steps they had taken to ensure product safety.

The "Pepsi Syringe Scare" serves as a cautionary tale of how quickly rumours can escalate and the profound impact on a company's reputation and consumer confidence. It underscores the necessity for companies to respond swiftly and transparently to such crises, employing all available means to clarify the facts and restore public trust.

The point of the company story is this: once you've understood the consequences of gossip and actively opt not to partake in its dissemination, all parties involved benefit. On top of all that, fixating so much on their perceived flaws takes our focus away from improving ourselves. Do not criticise others with the wrong intentions. Instead, reflect on your shortcomings and grow in patience, compassion, and forgiveness toward all. No one is perfect, so a little humility goes a long way when it comes to not judging those around us too harshly either.

Yes, gossip can be fun, but the truth is that it has no place in increasing likability. Gossip might seem harmless to bond with others at first, but it introduces toxicity. Even if our intentions aren't bad, the person on the receiving end understandably wonders what might be said about them when they're not around. This uncertainty eats away at relationships.

Gossip also skews negative perceptions. Why? Well, we don't have the full context and yet, we heavily judge others based on very little information. It is "normal" but should not be normalised. Over time, this damages how people view each other on a questionable level. Relationships require giving one another the benefit of the doubt, not forming judgments from one-sided stories alone.

Gossip spreads misinformation. Those little details get omitted or embellished each time a rumour passes from person to person. Many of us played Chinese Whispers as children, and though it was a game, it taught us that one comment is often misconstrued once passed to different people. Before long, the facts bearing on someone's reputation could be completely distorted from reality.

Gossip is also just plain unkind. Secretly criticising others behind their backs hurts their self-esteem when the talk inevitably gets back to them one way or another. Relationship success is never built on covertly tearing people down through private words.

Gossip does provide a fleeting sense of euphoria and it fosters a superficial connection through the illusion of shared secrets. But inevitably, trust erodes, replaced by suspicion and apprehension. One may find themselves unwittingly ensnared in the cycle of backstabbing rumours within closed social circles. Essentially, divisiveness is created, which leaves people unable to truly confide in each other, which subsequently destroys the genuine closeness that relationships require to deepen over time. Taking the high road requires discipline, and yet, those who do will reap the benefits of it. It undeniably takes a strong character to disengage from gossip.

Ultimately, life's greatest successes come from how well we connect with others, not how well we bring them down. Gossip damages not just others' reputations or self-worth but also our own character over time through association. So, to build strong, trusting relationships, it's worth consciously choosing to steer clear of even casual gossip whenever possible by focusing on each other's noble qualities instead. Our relationships and community benefit far more that way, and you should agree with me.

Strategies for Avoiding Gossip

Let's face it. People do not want to be judged or talked about behind their backs. We've all felt embarrassed or hurt when we found out others were making false accusations about us when we weren't around to defend ourselves. That is why we must show empathy, kindness, and respect toward others even when they're absent. The golden rule is a good guideline: don't say anything about someone you wouldn't say to their face.

If gossip comes up in conversation, one strategy is politely changing the subject to something more positive. You can say, "Oh, I don't feel comfortable discussing others who aren't here. How about playing that game last night instead?" Or "You know, conversations tend to go better when we don't judge people who aren't around to share their side. Anyway, should we watch that new movie?" Changing the subject light-heartedly like this lets others know gossip makes you uncomfortable without directly calling attention to or criticising it. You want to become a person to whom people will be uncomfortable spreading gossip.

People will often follow your lead if you redirect talk to more uplifting topics everyone can enjoy, like family, hobbies, current events, movies, or fun weekend plans. Smile and act engaged as you ask questions about the new subject to engage others in a more positive discussion. Try it out. You'll soon get better; you'll get better at smoothly and tactfully pivoting conversations away from malicious assessments of absent friends or coworkers.

Reframe conversations in a way that avoids criticism of anyone. For example, if others complain about a boss's behaviour, you can say, "It's a shame frustration came up. Every job has challenges; hopefully, things improve with open communication." Recasting situations in a less judgmental light and giving the benefit of the doubt helps conversations stay respectful.

KEEP YOUR HANDS CLEAN

You can also gently challenge gossip by playing the devil's advocate for the absent person. Calmly asking questions like "I wonder what their perspective is on that..." or "There may be more to the story; have you talked with them about it?" encourages reflecting on multiple sides instead of hastily judging someone who isn't there to represent themselves. Your friends will see you as fair-minded rather than someone who mindlessly participates in rumours.

Showing restraint is also wise. Keep your comments minimal, when others are gossiping. Let me be honest too: You may completely agree with everything the other person is saying but do not let this show. For example, rather than adding, "And I heard she yelled at her kids last weekend too!" you could say something mild like "Every family has their challenges" to prevent spreading rumours yourself or escalating negativity. Remember that minimising what you say does not make you weak; it shows strength, so do not let others convince you otherwise.

Additionally, lead by example by changing the subject to share encouraging interactions you've had with the party involved. Say something uplifting like, "To be fair, Mason did stay late to help me with a project the other day. I appreciated his offer to lend a hand." Leading with cheerful stories about people leaves less space in conversations for tearing others down. The aim is to become someone people don't gossip with because they know you won't entertain them. If you regularly bring positivity to discussions, eventually, others may follow your approach. Word of warning: You do not want to invalidate people's opinions if they genuinely wish to vent their frustrations about someone.

Pose As a Winner

To win friends, we must avoid condemning or judging people prematurely. People often make mistakes or see things differently based on their experiences. It's easy to think we have all the answers, but life does look different to different people.

Rather than prejudging, respectful people assume good intent until proven otherwise. They give others the benefit of the doubt and an opportunity to show their true character over time. Condemnation gets nowhere, but being open and non-threatening helps draw people out to connect on a deeper level. This lays the groundwork for real trust and friendship to form down the line.

If a new acquaintance does something you disagree with, avoid harsh reactions and show patience and interest in their perspective instead. Tactfully asking, "Can you tell me more about that?" acknowledges that there may be valid reasons behind actions, even if they don't appear that way at first glance. Respectfully hearing a thoughtful explanation with an open mind could change initial assumptions for the better.

No one is perfect. We all say or do questionable things at some point that we later regret. Give second chances instead of punishing minor slip-ups. Your compassionate spirit lets people

KEEP YOUR HANDS CLEAN

feel at ease opening up without fear of being defined by a single wrong move beneath their control.

Listen attentively too. Lead by example by showing interest in other people's experiences and sharing your own gracefully for perspective, not just broadcasting preconceptions. Make it a reciprocal discussion that uplifts each person's innate worth equally. Value humility by keeping an open mind; no one knows everything, and we can all show wisdom by thinking of how to lift ourselves up instead of putting ourselves down. This inclusive approach to respectfully engaging others will win you friendships wherever you go.

The unvarnished truth is condemning others gets you nowhere. It breeds resentment, not goodwill. But leading with compassion and giving people the benefit of the doubt to present their best, most authentic selves without fear of scorn invites openness and connection. It shows you respect individuals for who they are rather than labels or initial misconceptions. Mutual understanding and caring will develop into deep bonds worth cultivating. So, to make true friends, start by respecting others and suspending snap judgments in favour of patience to comprehend multiple viewpoints. Upholding inherent dignity and respect for humanity in each person you encounter will win you loyalty.

SPEAK WITH INFLUENCE

You know this already, but it serves as a great reminder. When talking with others, it's not just about what you say but how you say it. Your tone of voice, body language, eye contact, and other attributes shape how your message is received. Our tone influences others on an instinctual, emotional level that impacts how willing people are to engage with us. Of course, the words exchanged are important, but the delivery breathes life into a discussion and colours how people feel about you. So, it's worth paying close attention to tone and presence when conversing.

Use an engaging tone tailored to your audience and situation. Speak at a friendly, casual pace that shows you're relaxed and approachable. But remember to speed up if excitement about the topic naturally occurs. Expressing empathy may call for a gentler tone. Humour, too, can hold great power when applied correctly. You want listeners to feel your authentic passion coming through.

Being mindful of volume helps, too; whispering draws people close while shouting distances them. Most conversations thrive with an average volume where they can hear clearly without straining. If you're in a loud environment, subtly raise your tone for comfort without yelling. And adjust your pitch a little to avoid flat, lifeless tones that put others to sleep. Enliven topics through ups and downs in your vocal spirit.

Facial expressions that align with what you say also strongly influence perceptions. Smiling and appropriate eye contact between one-third and two-thirds of the time strengthens most relationships. But overdone grins look insincere, and avoiding eye contact signals disinterest. Make it a habit to reciprocate with others; match their energy levels, and they will feel unconsciously loved.

Posture speaks volumes, too— so sit or stand tall with open, inviting shoulder and body orientations toward others. Slouching closes you off, and fidgeting distracts you from the exchange. Nodding occasionally further reinforces engaged listening and understanding on your end. Sometimes, less is more, so avoid nodding excessively, as it could be perceived as a dishonest agreement. I trust you will find that perfect balance.

Gestures are used sparingly to emphasise aid delivery when natural. But flailing arms risks distraction or coming across as overly emotional. Therefore, relax your hands when not actively gesturing, and be mindful of differing cultural norms. The aim is to keep your physicality aligned with your message.

Speaking casually, without filler words, helps the conversation flow. Verbal ticks like "um," "you know," or ending statements with an abrupt question make listeners work harder to understand you. Another reminder is to avoid interrupting, and paraphrase their points to maintain mutual understanding. Delivery is an art perfected through self-awareness and practice.

Again, be mindful of all these cues as they create positive connections or missed opportunities for rapport. A friendly, upbeat tone makes people feel at ease and inspires openness. It signals to the listener that you view the interaction positively and want a cooperative discussion. And yet, a neutral or disinterested tone will bore others or make them disengage, all because it doesn't spark their interest or motivate them to listen. An angry, accusatory tone triggers defences and shuts all communication, implying criticism or attack.

Let me illustrate this: when business owners use a caring tone toward their employees, it boosts morale, job satisfaction, and productivity. However, an apathetic, harsh tone tends to damage performance. Employees want to feel valued rather than berated. Tone is essentially the nonverbal layer that weighs interactions.

Consider the tender exchanges between parents and their infants. When parents employ a happy, exaggerated sing-song voice, it not only captures the attention of their little ones but also fosters a nurturing environment conducive to their infant's development. Research suggests that this melodic tone stimulates key areas of the brain associated with language acquisition and emotional regulation. Remarkably, even children as young as six months old display an innate ability to discern tones of voice in others.

Our brains are wired from birth to subconsciously decode vocal tones as instinctual signals of safety or threat. This primal instinct serves as a survival mechanism, enabling us to navigate social interactions with heightened awareness and sensitivity. It's no wonder that within seconds of speaking to someone new, our tone begins forging positive or negative biases that shape its trajectory. A welcoming tone may elicit feelings of trust and connection, paving the way for meaningful rapport. In contrast, a cold or hostile tone can trigger a defensive response, leading to barriers in communication and rapport. The significance of tone in human interaction cannot be overstated. Therefore, the lesson still stands: utilise and adapt your tone for maximum results.

Of course, the tone alone does not solely determine interactions; what you say still carries significant weight. But, even when delivering the same message, versions spoken with different tones yield varied receptions. It can be the difference between inspiring others to consider a new business idea or putting them off the idea.

Tailoring your tone on the fly is a great ability. One that shows you understand diverse human dynamics and care about others' comfort levels. When speaking with kids, adopting a warmer, more excited vocal quality engages them more readily. Higher pitches with animated melodies grab youthful attention spans naturally. My advice is to remain sensitive to their emotions and shift to comforting, softer tones if they seem distressed. Avoid using scolding harshness, which risks shutting them down.

Similarly, consider using slightly clearer enunciation and louder volume around older adults to aid age-related hearing loss without talking down to them. Gauge each senior's preferences too; some prefer a spirited pep while others prefer a calmer style.

At formal business meetings, employ a composed yet confident vocal projection that commands appropriate authority. Around introverted acquaintances, modulate pacing and lower volume to avoid overwhelming them, leaving space for silences, too. In contrast, a more boisterous company calls for livelier energy. When interacting cross-culturally, educate yourself on different communication norms so as not to offend them unknowingly. Granted, this does come with practice and awareness.

With new friends, prioritise natural warmth and enthusiasm to accelerate comfort during early social interactions. Remember, to let close companions experience the entirety of your personality. Neither approach is better; both have benefits contextually.

Communicating good or bad news warrants nuanced delivery. Doctors inform their loved one their relatives have passed away with compassion. Parents inform their children they are going on holiday with excitement. Spouses propose to their partners with joy. I'm sure you get the point, yet most people are unaware of the sensitivity and adaptability needed.

Once you have perfected your delivery, you can strive in any conversation. The three key elements are pitch, volume, and pace, which all significantly shape how your message lands. Tailoring these factors can transform your communication effectiveness from mediocre to magnetic. Let's examine each in more detail.

We naturally vary pitch in our conversations to add expression and emphasis. Yet, it also influences how engaged listeners feel—so when we speak in a dull monotone without variation, it risks putting others to sleep. Fluctuating pitches erratically may seem weird. Find the right balance, and you will excel.

Maintaining a predominantly moderate pitch while purposefully fluctuating up or down at appropriate moments keeps people focused. You often see this attribute in successful motivational speakers. Raising the pitch for more exciting sections, then lowering it for softer parts, builds dramatic intrigue.

Volume is another engagement booster. We often fail to realise how loud or soft we speak, so gauge an average volume to allow for comfortable listening. Whispering draws people close but risks them missing out while shouting distances them with sensory overload or irritation if the tone feels angry.

Similarly, lowering at certain pauses builds suspense, waiting for the revealing rise again. Remember, always respect different processing volumes based on disabilities or preferences. Overall, volume control keeps people optimally involved.

Pace also deserves thought. Rushing through without pausing risks overwhelming others or sounding undesirably anxious. Conversely, dragging too slowly loses their interest quickly as well. Find a rhythm and tailor it to each person.

Speed up when vibing off others' energy, and slow down when giving sensitive news so they absorb each moment. Accelerate to build up to the punchline. Speak passionately without forced hype, keeping everyone on the same wavelength.

Mastering all three adds orchestration. It's an instinctual art of drawing others in and keeping them glued, where pure words sometimes fall short. After all, we're all naturally hardwired to feel the impassioned emotion behind the words expressed. Also, make it a habit to welcome feedback from others because constant improvement comes through humility, not arrogance.

Avoiding Awkward Silences

It's natural for brief pauses to happen as you digest what was said or allow space for a response. Remember that dragging on too long is awkward, and those weird silences risk making both parties uncomfortable. Lulls that seem like no one knows what to say next end up stifling the flow of interaction. Lucky for us, with some conscious guidance, you can steer conversations past such uneasy gaps by learning when silence serves and when it hinders us.

Recognising that short, considerate silences enhance bonding when followed by honest sharing. While aimless, open-ended gaps where people stare or await rescue from the other side create social unease. So, having strategies ready to fill lulls reassuringly becomes handy here without forcing artificial verbosity.

By offering follow-up questions directed at the other person, you may allow them to continue the conversation easily by sharing their viewpoints. For example, "That's fascinating; I'd love to hear more about how you got into that line of work" shows curiosity without pressure to supply your reaction immediately. Simple prompts like "And how about you? Any similar experiences?" likewise shift attention helpfully.

When all else fails, steer conversations to a related topic that you both already find intriguing. "You know, this reminds me..." "Did you manage to secure the Wimbledon tickets?" "I always thought it would be great fun to watch." This effortlessly redirects mutually engaging discussions without breaking the flow altogether.

Of course, we must understand that true silences remain necessary for reflection. Learning when these healthy or awkward types occur requires compassionately observing others' comfort levels through their body language and expressions. Remember, some individuals process internally more than externally. Your role becomes not filling silences by default but perceptively addressing social unease subtly if it arises.

LEARN TO KEEP YOUR WORD

Trust plays a pivotal role in every relationship, whether personal or professional. It takes time to build but can be broken instantly if not handled carefully. One of the foundations of trust is following through on commitments and keeping your word. Talk less and do more. People will be sceptical if you tell them how great you are at keeping your word. Show it through your actions instead. Do not promise greatness and deliver mediocrity. You must instead underpromise and overdeliver. So then, people will feel empowered around you because they will feel you're exceeding their expectations.

We've likely all been in situations where someone disappointed us by not doing what they said. Maybe a friend bailed on plans at the last minute, or promised work wasn't finished by a deadline. It's disappointing, and that person is now perceived as unreliable. Even for small things, breaking your word chips away at faith in your character. Over time, a track record of not following through poisons relationships and stops progress.

Conversely, think of relationships where the other person consistently delivers as promised. Don't we feel we can depend on them and that their bond is stable? A history of word-keeping fosters an environment where partners can freely share and depend on their commitments. Understand: Those who succeed at keeping their word are the ones who control the number of commitments they agree to. They never take on more than they are emotionally or physically able to. Many people are often motivated by the need to please others by proving their dedication - the issue is that they overestimated their capabilities at that moment. Be humble when you exceed your own expectations. Do not allow temporary success to create an egotistical mentality. The solution is to set a realistic goal, and when you reach it, stop and evaluate. Belief in momentum will only make you emotional and delay strategic thinking.

Some feel commitments are flexible if life gets busy or distracting. But this mindset only breeds uncertainty for the other party. Prioritising duties shows the relationship is valued as much as any passing urge. And yet, broken promises, however minor, leave folks questioning how firm a bond truly is, so learning discipline makes all the difference.

It's also about being accountable—not making excuses when fallible but owning errors with humility. Saying "I'm sorry, I'll do better" is reassuring versus angering people further with finger-pointing. Admitting mistakes is admirable because it shows insight into the growth needed while still honouring initial responsibilities. Forgiveness then follows to mend and strengthen the connection on a new footing.

The commitment could be anything from completing a work project to making time for someone dealing with difficulties to even keeping a dinner date agreement arranged weeks ago. Whatever the agreement, big or small, faithful parties should remember why it matters. They don't dismiss or forget their given word but think of the other's well-being and trust, relying on the union. This shared perspective on honouring relationships at their core keeps all parties committed for the long run.

Integrity should never take a backseat to fleeting pressures. True care demands owning the duty to fulfil roles freely declared and accepted. Holding oneself accountable—humbly admitting flaws but learning from them— will allow you to excel.

Strategies for Keeping Your Word

Keeping promises and staying true to our word is important for building trust in relationships. However, unintentionally breaking commitments is easy if we're not careful. Here are some strategies anyone can use to avoid losing credibility:

- One key is learning not to make promises we may struggle to keep. We've all been in a pinch, wanting to sound helpful, so we offer to do something without fully considering if it's realistic given our other duties. Then, when we can't deliver, it harms trust. So, instead of giving an automatic "yes," pause and thoughtfully assess your abilities is okay. If something seems iffy, it's better to honestly say, "Let me check my schedule and get back to you." This preserves your reputation for reliability.

- Similarly, we sometimes stretch the truth to sound impressive in a conversation. But vague boasts usually backfire when not fulfilled. It's much better to say what you know than to proclaim things to gain attention or approval. Over time, the truth rings clear while exaggerated claims are uncovered. Your character shines through real discussions, not superficial comments made just because.

- When uncertain if a promise can be kept, communicate upfront and work out an understanding with the other party rather than hoping things change suddenly. Most people will appreciate open discussion over feeling let down secretly. Together, find an alternative, like partially delivering now with full completion later once capacity clears up.

- If delays still occur on agreements through no fault of your own, promptly explain the situation respectfully. Admitting problems humbly and pursuing fairness reassures people you still care about fulfilling duties, even if factors outside your control postpone the timeline. Continued updates maintain trust if respect and the effort to remedy it are clear.

- When able to follow through, do so with excellence and enthusiasm rather than begrudgingly hitting the basics. Going above and beyond demonstrates how much keeping your word means to you. It could be a heartfelt thank you for someone's patience or a small extra thanks for their ongoing faith. Your whole attitude radiates the importance of commitment to you.

- Don't take on too many obligations at once. We all want to help others, but overloading our plates risks dropping balls. Know your limits and when to decline offers graciously. Distributing responsibilities ensures promises stay manageable and confidence in your word remains unbroken.

- If glitches occur, admit your mistakes respectfully without making excuses rather than angering others further. A soft "I'm sorry, I messed up" conveys humility and care to regain trust versus bitter defence. Make amends sincerely, however possible, if another party suffers harm from relying on your commitment.

LEARN TO KEEP YOUR WORD

Under promise and Overdeliver

Nothing destroys trust faster than promising great things but only providing mediocrity or letting others down. That is why the wise approach is to underpromise yet strive to overdeliver consistently whenever possible.

We've all been in situations where someone hyped something up beyond reason. Maybe a friend swore their party would be epic, yet it was dull. Or a salesperson vowed an item could do wonders when it was lacklustre. In both cases, getting less than what was promised leaves people feeling misled and questioning the person's honesty or competence going forward. Why take their word seriously now if exaggerated claims don't materialise?

The ego may want drastic hype for praise or money, but it damages integrity in the long run. Your sincerity and character remain solid by moderately setting expectations yet astonishing others positively. It's far better to have a history of happily surprising partners than bitter memories of letdowns from impractical exaggerations.

Some argue mediocrity is fine if goals are low-balled severely. But minimum standards are no way to win loyalty or affection. Striving higher shows how much you value adding brightness to a relationship versus idle claims of help that dissolve into half-hearted medians.

So, whether it's completing projects for work, spending quality time with loved ones, or helping others through difficult periods, under promise what seems achievable and preferably deliver more through passionate care, even something small, like bringing home a surprise treat, illustrates that the priority is upholding others' well-being through sincerity, not recognition alone. Thoughtful acts build reputations as people who brightly enhance lives, not disappointment.

Consider people's emotions and how downgraded promises still sting pride, even if technically met. Life has uncertainties, so dependability built from the steady exceeding of downplayed vows sees partners as a united team. No one falters alone when surrounded by people who improve their worlds remarkably each step of the way out of adoration, not self-indulgence. Such gracious spirits become beacons of comfort for all around them.

CONCLUSION

Well, friends, we've come to the end of our time learning how to become a people magnet. I pray these chapters gave you some ideas on conversing with others and increasing likability. If you read this book throughout and learned very little, I will consider it a complete failure.

Talking with people is mighty important in life. Whether you're making new pals, visiting close friends, or meeting folks for work, how we talk to each other matters. This book covered many things, like making a good first impression, smiling and listening when others speak. Finding things, you agree on makes chatting easier. Avoid silly fights, and disagree nicely. Ask questions to learn more about others. Give compliments since they feel good to hear. Learn to remember names so people know you care. Keep the talks interesting so they don't get boring. Don't brag too much or share private things too soon. Show yourself slowly when trust is built, and get along with different people by adjusting how you act.

But most importantly, you should treat all people with kindness and respect, even if you disagree. Calmly talking through differences fixes more than yelling. And if you're upset, take a breath before talking so you don't say something you regret. Feelings of anger often come from being scared or hurting, so empathise with what others feel, too.

Some things that stuck with me were being reliable and doing what you say. Your reputation takes time to build, like savings in a bank, but it can be lost fast. Express your sincere thanks for both big and small favours. Few things are more important than expressing gratitude. People feel good knowing they matter. Ask follow-up questions to show you care about their interests. Listen instead of just waiting to speak.

When disagreeing, try to understand different views without fighting. Peaceful discussions where all sides feel heard work better for solving problems. And don't gossip or say unnecessary remarks, as that damages friendships. Also, end talks on an upbeat note when possible. Chat about fun times, dreams, and things you learn. Ask others to share, too. Laughter and optimism are catchy, so bring more of that spirit to how you connect.

I pray this has helped you to become better at winning friends and increasing your likability. Lastly, be kind. You never know what opportunities can arise when you are sincere. I wish you the best in talking to anyone about anything.

Love,

Caleb Luke

Thank You

You made it to the end! You could have chosen any other book, but you took a chance on mine, and I seriously appreciate that.

Before you go, could you please consider posting a review on Amazon? Posting a review is the easiest way to support my work an independent author.

Got questions? Contact me personally at support@caleb.co.uk

UK   USA

REFERENCES

Anien, T. S. (2019, October 5). *Smiles are important for better communication: Experts*. Deccan Herald. https://www.deccanherald.com/india/karnataka/bengaluru/smiles-are-important-for-better-communication-experts-766028.html

Ashenden, P. (2020, February 18). *Nonverbal communication: How body language and nonverbal cues are key*. Lifesize. https://www.lifesize.com/blog/speaking-without-words/

Boogaard, K. (2016, September 29). *6 smart ways to disagree with someone respectfully*. Inc.com. https://www.inc.com/kat-boogaard/6-key-tips-to-respectfully-disagree-with-someone.html

Booher Research Institute. (2017, August 29). *How to skip small talk and get to know someone*. https://booherresearch.com/skip-small-talk-get-know-someone/

Cherry, K. (2023, March 15). *First impressions: Everything you need to make a good introduction*. Verywell Mind. https://www.verywellmind.com/make-a-good-first-impression-7197993

REFERENCES

Cirino, E. (2018). *Want to make a great first impression? Give these tips a try.* Healthline. https://www.healthline.com/health/first-impressions

Everett, J. A. C., Faber, N. S., & Crockett, M. (2015). Preferences and beliefs in ingroup favoritism. *Frontiers in Behavioral Neuroscience, 9*(15). https://doi.org/10.3389/fnbeh.2015.00015

Fritscher, L. (2019). *How to be vulnerable.* Verywell Mind. https://www.verywellmind.com/fear-of-vulnerability-2671820

Frost, A. (2020, June 19). *10 ways to become a better conversationalist.* The Muse. https://www.themuse.com/advice/10-ways-to-become-a-better-conversationalist

Gruen, M. (2021, March 2). *Why keeping your word is the best way to show respect.* Rolling Stone. https://www.rollingstone.com/culture-council/articles/keeping-word-show-respect-1131595/

Holland, M. G. (1996). What's Wrong with Telling the Truth? An Analysis of Gossip. *American Philosophical Quarterly, 33*(2), 197–209. https://www.jstor.org/stable/20009858

Houston, E. (2019, April 9). *How to express gratitude to others: 19 examples and ideas.* PositivePsychology. https://positivepsychology.com/how-to-express-gratitude/

Hyatt, M. (2010, March 17). *Keeping your word.* Full Focus. https://fullfocus.co/keeping-your-word/

Landsman, I. (2023, May 23). *Understanding "tone" and its impact on conversations.* Helpspot. https://www.helpspot.com/blog/tone-impact-on-conversations

Lonczak, H. (2021, May 29). *How to build rapport with clients: 18 examples and questions.* PositivePsychology. https://positivepsychology.com/rapport-building/

Manning, M. (2018, September 3). *Let's revive the lost art of communication… we can do it together!* Sixty and Me. https://sixtyandme.com/lets-revive-the-lost-art-of-communication-we-can-do-it-together/

Miles, M. (2022, April 26). *How to build rapport: 6 tactics to build strong relationships.* BetterUp. https://www.betterup.com/blog/how-to-build-rapport

Mind Tools Content Team. (n.d.). *Keeping Your Word at Work.* Mind Tools. https://www.mindtools.com/awtninu/keeping-your-word-at-work

REFERENCES

Nienaber, A.-M., Hofeditz, M., & Romeike, P. D. (2015). Vulnerability and trust in leader-follower relationships. *Personnel Review, 44*(4), 567–591. https://doi.org/10.1108/pr-09-2013-0162

Orlowska, A. B., Krumhuber, E. G., Rychlowska, M., & Szarota, P. (2018). Dynamics matter: Recognition of reward, affiliative, and dominance smiles from dynamic vs. static displays. *Frontiers in Psychology, 9.* https://doi.org/10.3389/fpsyg.2018.00938

Overton, A., & Lowry, A. (2013). Conflict management: Difficult conversations with difficult people. *Clinics in Colon and Rectal Surgery, 26*(04), 259–264. NCBI. https://doi.org/10.1055/s-0033-1356728

Sansone, R. A., & Sansone, L. A. (2010). Gratitude and well being: The benefits of appreciation. *Psychiatry (Edgmont (Pa. : Township)), 7*(11), 18–22. https://www.ncbi.nlm.nih.gov/pmc/articles/PMC3010965/

The Social Skills Center. (2022, May 2). *Why your tone of voice is so important.* https://socialskillscenter.com/why-your-tone-of-voice-is-so-important/

Ullah, R., Zada, M., Saeed, I., Khan, J., Shahbaz, M., Vega-Muñoz, A., & Salazar-Sepúlveda, G. (2021). Have you heard that—"gossip"? Gossip spreads rapidly and influences broadly. *International Journal of Environmental Research*

and Public Health, 18(24), 13389.
https://doi.org/10.3390/ijerph182413389

Wargo, E. (2006). How Many Seconds to a First Impression? *APS Observer, 19*(7).
https://www.psychologicalscience.org/observer/how-many-seconds-to-a-first-impression

Wellineux. (2018, March 21). *Reviving the dying art of meaningful conversation.*
https://www.wellineux.com/blog/2018/3/reviving-the-dying-art-of-meaningful-conversation

Printed in Dunstable, United Kingdom